Cooperative Threat Reduction for a New Era

James E. Goodby, Daniel L. Burghart, Cheryl A. Loeb
and Charles L. Thornton

Center for Technology and National Security Policy

National Defense University

September 2004

James E. Goodby has been professionally involved with nuclear issues for 50 years. He served in ambassadorial assignments in the administrations of Presidents Carter, Reagan, and Clinton and was chief negotiator for Nunn-Lugar agreements with Russia, Ukraine, Kazakhstan, and Belarus in 1993-94.

Daniel L. Burghart joined the Center for Technology and National Security Policy in July 2003 after his retirement from the United States Army as a Colonel. He was a member of the Faculty of the National War College from July 2000 to 2003 and is a specialist in Russian and Central European Affairs.

Cheryl A. Loeb is a research associate at the Center for Technology and National Security Policy at the National Defense University and is also currently pursuing a Ph.D. in Biodefense at George Mason University. Ms. Loeb may be contacted via e-mail at loebc@ndu.edu or by phone at (202) 685-2397.

Charles L. Thornton is currently a research fellow at the Center for International and Security Studies in the School of Public Policy at the University of Maryland, where he is also pursuing a Ph.D. in international security policy. Mr. Thornton continues to consult for the government on nuclear threat reduction cooperation issues.

Defense & Technology Papers *are published by the National Defense University Center for Technology and National Security Policy, Fort Lesley J. McNair, Washington, DC. CTNSP publications are available online at* http://www.ndu.edu/ctnsp/publications.html.

Executive Summary

1. The United States and the international community are engaged in a campaign that will determine whether nuclear weapons will inexorably become an indispensable weapon for nations around the world. An important new part of that campaign will be directed at preventing international terrorist organizations from acquiring nuclear materials or nuclear weapons. The highest priority in this campaign is securing all of the highly enriched uranium (HEU) in this country and abroad. This is the material from which terrorists could most easily make a rudimentary atomic bomb capable of inflicting catastrophic damage in any large American city.

2. A global approach is needed to secure all nuclear weapons, as well as HEU, plutonium, and other fissile materials, to safeguard against illicit nuclear weapons programs, trafficking, and terrorism. Several initiatives launched by the Bush administration address this need. CTR funding from the United States and other donors should be used for some of these initiatives, especially UN Security Council Resolution 1540, which calls for global cooperation in strengthening safeguards over nuclear materials.

3. Overcoming obstacles such as liability and other legal and political issues that have seriously hindered progress in the U.S.–Russian CTR partnership in recent years should be a high priority. It will take a summit meeting between the Russian and American presidents to overcome the current obstacles to accelerated progress in securing nuclear stockpiles in Russia. One objective of such a summit meeting should be to review a comprehensive report on the status of all U.S.–Russian CTR programs and to decide what steps need to be taken to accelerate and sustain the joint effort.

4. North Korea and probably Iran are in the process of building overt nuclear arsenals, complete with ballistic missile delivery systems. This could trigger an avalanche of national decisions to acquire nuclear weapons in Asia, the Middle East, and elsewhere. In this case, the Nuclear Nonproliferation Treaty (NPT) could become a dead letter. The concepts and techniques developed by the Nunn-Lugar Cooperative Threat Reduction (CTR) program could be useful in helping to achieve nonproliferation goals in those countries. Moreover, joint CTR projects could have a positive effect on broader country-to-country relationships.

5. As the number of nuclear-armed states increases, there will be a corresponding increase in the possibility that nuclear weapons will be stolen or detonated accidentally, or that miscalculations will trigger a nuclear exchange. There were close calls during the Cold War, despite enormous efforts made to avoid accidents, miscalculation, or loss of control. The same should be expected with fledgling nuclear weapon states. India and Pakistan are cases in point. Although a program of cooperation must begin with modest first steps, the application of CTR techniques, with or without the participation of the United States, could be helpful to both nations. Any agreements reached by the United States with these countries should be in the context of broader U.S. security and foreign policy goals, both regionally and globally. The CTR program has helped protect the world against the catastrophe that could have happened as a nuclear-armed superpower, the Soviet Union, collapsed. Despite these successes, there is much still to be done in Russia and elsewhere in the territory of the former Soviet Union.

6. Resources should not be a large problem in India and Pakistan, as programs could proceed incrementally with low-cost measures. North Korea and Iran pose greater needs for resources for dismantling nuclear facilities and meeting energy requirements, but here the more difficult obstacles are likely to be the unwillingness of these countries to cooperate. The administration is working with other nations in both cases, and the costs involved should be shared among partner nations. Global initiatives, such as the Proliferation Security Initiative, UN Security Resolution 1540, the G8 Global Partnership Against the Spread of Weapons and Materials of Mass Destruction, and the Global Threat Reduction Initiative, could also require substantial resources, but these proposals are multilateral in their nature, and costs could be shared. Resources should not be a limiting factor in the expansion of CTR programs beyond the former Soviet Union.

7. The antiproliferation campaign now consists of three tiers of programs and policies: those inherited from the Cold War period (e.g., the NPT); those put in place as the first response to changed circumstances after the Cold War, including the Nunn–Lugar program; and initiatives taken during the Bush administration to establish a global and regional antiproliferation regime. There is a need for better integration of these programs at top levels of government.

8. The 9/11 Commission recommended a major overhaul of the way the U.S. Government is organized for intelligence. It recommended a "joint unified command concept" and foresaw the need for "national intelligence centers that combine experts from all the collection disciplines to be directed against common targets—such as counter-terrorism or nuclear proliferation." The same organizational problems exist in the nation's antiproliferation programs and policies and improvements in that area should accompany the reform of the nation's intelligence functions. To paraphrase the 9/11 Commission, organizational reforms in the antiproliferation field should enable a single authority to influence the leadership and the budgets of the antiproliferation operating arms of the Departments of Defense, Energy, Homeland Security, and State, as well as the relevant operations of the CIA, FBI, and Customs Service.

Table of Contents

I. Introduction to Cooperative Threat Reduction

What Has Been Done

One of the greatest challenges to both national and international security stems from the threat posed by weapons of mass destruction, especially nuclear weapons. In 1991, Senators Sam Nunn (D-GA) and Richard Lugar (R-IN) authored and advocated the Soviet Nuclear Threat Reduction Act after the breakup of the Soviet Union (creating what is now commonly referred to as Nunn–Lugar Cooperative Threat Reduction [CTR] program).[1] The program currently receives funding of over $1 billion a year for cooperative activities to secure and eliminate weapons of mass destruction and related materials and technologies in the former Soviet Union.

The Nunn–Lugar CTR program can rightly be called the Marshall Plan of nuclear nonproliferation. It was one of the primary instruments available to the United States for dealing with the dangerous situation resulting from the collapse of the Soviet Union in 1991. Problems still exist, however, with regard to the safe and secure storage and handling of nuclear materials in Russia. Substantial resources from the United States and other nations will continue to be needed to eliminate these potential threats in the future. However, the mutual dedication to problem solving that has, at the best of times, characterized the Nunn–Lugar program is now missing. As a result, secondary issues and other priorities have prevented further progress from being made.

The early stages of the Nunn–Lugar program, understandably, were marked by suspicion and a lack of trust on both sides—attitudes that hindered progress and slowed implementation of agreed-on measures. Further complicating the situation was that the breakup of the Soviet Union also meant the breakup of the unified control system that facilitated expeditious execution of directives from above. The Yeltsin government was notorious for unfulfilled commitments, and as a result, those working the various programs found that agreed-on procedures often had to be renegotiated at each intervening level of the bureaucracy before they could be put into effect. Even such seemingly simple issues as

---

[1] For the purposes of this report, "Nunn–Lugar" and "CTR" refer to programs managed by the U.S. Departments of Defense (DOD), Energy (DOE), State (DOS), and Commerce (DOC), as well as their counterpart agencies in the former Soviet Union. Although CTR is the official name only of the DOD program, there is no other convenient moniker with which to refer to all U.S. government efforts in this area.

whether taxes had to be paid on materials provided free of charge under CTR continue to cause problems to this day. To the credit of both sides, in previous years, when a problem was encountered, efforts were made to come up with workable solutions, rather than allowing the process to fall into a series of mutual recriminations. In spite of this record, the program has become bogged down in recent years over issues such as liability for damages and other essentially secondary matters.

In terms of nuclear weapons, some 6,382 nuclear warheads have been deactivated under CTR. These include all armaments from the former Soviet republics of Belarus, Kazakhstan, and Ukraine, where the weapons' status and security came into serious question after the breakup of the Soviet Union. More than 1,400 delivery systems, including ballistic missiles, cruise missiles, submarines, and strategic bombers have been decommissioned or destroyed.[2] In terms of materials that could be used to create weapons, over 200 metric tons of highly enriched uranium (HEU) has been eliminated. Security in transport and storage, and accountability of both weapons and weapon materials, has been enhanced. Finally, more than 22,000 scientists formerly employed in weapons programs (chemical and biological included) have been shifted to cooperative, peaceful endeavors.[3] In sum, the world is a safer place today because of the efforts of the Nunn–Lugar program.

What Must Be Done

The Nunn–Lugar program directly addresses the gravest danger the nation faces: nuclear-armed terrorists. If terrorist organizations were to acquire HEU in sufficient quantity, and had the technical expertise, it would not be difficult for them to build a primitive, but deadly, nuclear device. The first priority of the United States and its upstream homeland security efforts must be to prevent that from happening.

Up to two-thirds of Russia's weapons-grade material remains inadequately secured. According to the DOE, at the end of Fiscal Year (FY) 2003, comprehensive security upgrades had been completed on only 22 percent of the estimated 600 metric tons of estimated nuclear-weapons-usable material in Russia. Rapid security upgrades had been put

---

[2] Defense Threat Reduction Agency, "CTR Scorecard," 21 July 2004 <http://www.dtra.mil/toolbox/directorates/ctr/scorecard.cfm.>
[3] Senator Richard G. Lugar, "Nunn–Lugar Accomplishments," <http://lugar.senate.gov/nunnlugar html>.

in place on only 42 percent of this material.[4] While U.S. and NATO forces in Europe are being restructured, it may be an opportune time for the United States and Russia to take up the issue of control over tactical nuclear weapons. Although it is essential that existing materials be secured, attention must also be paid to facilities capable of producing more weapons-grade materials in the future. Three nuclear reactors in Russia currently produce approximately 1.2 metric tons of weapons-grade plutonium each year. In addition, there are concerns about reactor safety in general and about the need to convert reactors using HEU to use lower-enriched fuels. Finally, although CTR has worked to decommission strategic submarines that carry ballistic missiles, nonstrategic submarines that are capable of launching nuclear capable cruise missiles, which themselves possess propulsion systems with highly enriched fuels, have not been addressed. The priority among these tasks, however, must be securing HEU.

Purpose of the Study

The purpose of this study is to review the techniques developed and used by the Nunn–Lugar program to date, including some closely related activities, and to recommend specific ways in which these techniques could be applied on a global basis to eliminate the various types of nuclear threats faced by the United States. Expanding the scope of the Nunn–Lugar CTR program beyond Russia should not jeopardize the political support for funding CTR. Rather, as a recent Carnegie Endowment report has emphasized, nuclear proliferation has become a global problem. Thus, the United States should be willing to take the lead in managing an expanded CTR initiative at the same time it encourages participation by other nations.[5]

Five categories of nuclear threat reduction will be discussed in this article:

1. Residual nuclear-related security problems in Russia.
2. Nuclear weapons programs in de facto nuclear weapon states. India and Pakistan are the two cases in this category.

---

[4] Department of Energy, "FY 2005 Congressional Budget Request," February 2004 <http://www.mbe.doe.gov/budget/05budget/content/NNSAADM/nnsasum.pdf>.
[5] Carnegie Endowment for International Peace. "Universal Compliance: A Strategy for Nuclear Security," June 2004 <http://wmd.ceip.matrixgroup.net/UniversalCompliance.pdf>.

3. Applying CTR techniques in the cases of former noncooperative states. This category will examine the case of Libya, a former proliferating state, which is in the process of dismantling its weapons of mass destruction program.
4. Nuclear weapons programs in noncooperative states. North Korea and Iran are the two cases that will be examined in this category.
5. Insecure storage of fissionable materials in countries around the world. A global clean-out approach is required to deal with these situations.

As the Nunn–Lugar program proceeded from concept to programmatic action in the early 1990s, a growing set of agreements with Russia, Belarus, Kazakhstan, and Ukraine began to shape a series of generic tools that were brought to bear on the nuclear threat. Broadly speaking, the objectives of this assemblage of tools included:

- Destruction and Dismantlement: eliminating the means of delivering nuclear weapons, principally ballistic missiles.
- Managerial Control: ensuring the safe and secure custody of nuclear weapons and nuclear materials under the control of governmentally authorized organizations.
- Nonproliferation: preventing the illicit leakage of nuclear weapons, nuclear materials, and nuclear technology to other nations or terrorist groups.

It should be noted at the outset that these broad goals of CTR are not always congruent with goals appropriate to some of the cases we will discuss. Preserving the chain of custody for nuclear weapons is not a current U.S. goal in the case of North Korea, for example, because the goal is, rather, to eliminate all vestiges of a nuclear weapons program.

II. CTR—A Brief History

The impetus for threat reduction arose in the aftermath of the failed coup attempt in the Soviet Union in August 1991. Senators Sam Nunn and Richard Lugar proposed an amendment to the Conventional Armed Forces in Europe (CFE) Treaty, which became the Soviet Nuclear Threat Reduction Act of 1991. This act authorized the use of $400 million from FY 1992 DOD funds to assist in destroying nuclear, chemical, and other weapons; to transport, store, and safeguard such weapons in conjunction with their destruction; and to establish verifiable safeguards against the proliferation of such weapons. In 1993, the program became known as the Nunn–Lugar CTR program and received direct funding into its own budget line item, rather than having DOD move funds budgeted for other activities into the CTR program. At this time, experts from other government agencies, especially Energy, State, and Commerce, were brought in where their expertise was needed. In 1997, each of these agencies took management and budgetary responsibility for the projects they were associated with.

Although getting off to a slow start, as a result of, among other reasons, bureaucratic intransigence and lingering mistrust on both sides, the program evolved as procedures were worked out and institutionalized and as umbrella agreements were negotiated with each of the states receiving assistance. In the 1990s, the program was given a boost by the establishment of the Gore–Chernomyrdin Commission, which tracked the progress of a number of joint Russian–American projects, including CTR. As a result of this visibility, funding for CTR increased throughout the 1990s, and with the overcoming of procedural obstacles, results began to be achieved. The Defense against Weapons of Mass Destruction Act (Nunn–Lugar–Domenici legislation), passed by Congress on 23 September 1996, can be considered the second stage of the Nunn–Lugar CTR program.[6] The Nunn–Lugar–Domenici Act was aimed at domestic preparedness and charged federal departments and agencies with putting systems into place that would protect the public against terrorists.[7]

Although questions were raised by members of the Bush administration about the efficacy of the Nunn–Lugar program, a White House/National Security Council review of the

---

[6] In this report we identify three stages of Nunn–Lugar CTR as a way to show the evolution of the program.
[7] Federation of American Scientists, "Domestic Preparedness," 30 January 1999
<http://www.fas.org/spp/starwars/program/domestic htm>.

program and its achievements, combined with the aftermath of September 11, led to an expanded CTR program to support the war on terrorism in 2003. The expanded program is considered the third stage of the Nunn–Lugar program and was incorporated in the FY 2003 Defense Authorization Bill. It included an amendment that would strengthen U.S. efforts to secure nuclear and radiological materials in the former Soviet Union to prevent their acquisition and use by terrorists.[8] The expansion of the CTR program authorized the use of $50 million of CTR funds a year for emergency nonproliferation activities outside of the former Soviet Union and provided $5 million for expanding the Materials Protection, Control, and Accounting (MPC&A) program to countries outside the former Soviet Union. It also provided $5 million to study options for assisting other countries in improving their export control programs, including of materials that could be used in nuclear or radiological dispersal devices.[9]

Even though this third stage of Nunn–Lugar provided the foundation and impetus for applying CTR techniques and tools to countries outside of the former Soviet Union, this program has not yet been applied outside of Russia and the former Soviet states, despite the evident need. CTR concepts and techniques should be applied in India, Pakistan, Libya, North Korea, and Iran if circumstances permit. It should be underscored that the application of CTR techniques does not necessarily imply that the United States will become the chief negotiator and provider of funds for all activities. It is the techniques, first and foremost, rather than the sponsor that should be examined for their relevance to problems that may threaten international security.

Methods Developed in the Former Soviet Union

Based on a listing of goals and programs defined by the Defense Threat Reduction Agency (DTRA),[10] and on a similar list covering all U.S. government agencies, developed by

---

[8] Council for a Livable World, "Senate Defense Authorization Bill Strengthens and Expands Non-Proliferation Efforts," 9 July 2002 <http://www.clw.org/control/prolifbill html>.
[9] Ibid.
[10] Defense Threat Reduction Program, "Threat Reduction Programs," <http://www.dtra.mil/toolbox/directorates/ctr/programs/index.cfm>, accessed 20 September 2004.

the Nuclear Threat Initiative (NTI),[11] the list below is a simplified description of tools that were used in the former Soviet Union to deal with nuclear threats.[12]

1. Improving physical control of items of interest
2. Removing nuclear weapons, fissile materials, and equipment for producing weapons-useable fissile material from countries of concern
3. Improving accounting for items of interest
4. Diverting technical and scientific expertise to civilian purposes
5. Preventing the leakage of technology to unauthorized recipients
6. Preventing the export of nuclear weapons, materials and equipment
7. Eliminating means of delivering nuclear weapons
8. Hardening transportation links against attack
9. Assisting in the conversion of defense industries and weapons laboratories to civilian operations
10. Rendering irreversible, to the extent possible, the dismantlement of excess nuclear warheads
11. Supporting alternative power sources in order to block the production of nuclear materials which could be used in nuclear weapons
12. Converting weapons-useable fissile materials into fuels for civilian and commercial power needs
13. Purchasing highly enriched uranium for re-sale as fuel for commercial nuclear power plants

Table 1 – Generic List of CTR Tools

Categories of Threat Reduction

For the purpose of this report, there are five categories of nuclear threat reduction to which these tools can be applied. The first category looks at Russia. There are also several candidate nations to which CTR could be expanded as part of the antiproliferation effort, including category 2, which consists of nuclear states that would willingly accept CTR efforts under the right cooperative and diplomatic circumstances as part an overall effort to

---

[11] Nuclear Threat Initiative, "Controlling Nuclear Warheads and Materials," <http://nti.org/e_research/cnwm/overview/cnwm_home.asp>, accessed 20 September 2004.
[12] The reader should be aware that not all of these methods were funded by the Nunn–Lugar program. Furthermore, when the term "nuclear threat" is used in this study, it does not necessarily refer to the current intentions of the government that owns nuclear weapons or materials.

limit the spread of nuclear capabilities and materials. Category 3 includes former hostile states that are now cooperating in disarmament and who possess either materials or technology that could prove dangerous if they fall into the hands of terrorists. Category 4 consists of nations with nuclear programs, and possibly weapons, that have been hostile to external efforts to monitor their programs, but who might accept CTR assistance in return for international incentives and, more specifically, international aid. Category 5 looks at the threat from unsecured HEU around the world and the global effort to secure quantities of fissionable materials.

III. HEU Terrorism

The end of the Cold War and its global superpower confrontation signaled a transition in national and international security priorities away from high-alert nuclear weapons and massive deterrent operations and toward a focus on the managerial control over the global stockpile of warheads and fissionable materials. Successive analytical and media reports have highlighted the threats posed by nondeployed nuclear warheads and their explosive materials: plutonium and HEU.[13] Moreover, the practice of international terrorism has undergone a paradigm shift: It appears that new types of substate organizations have formed that seek to inflict mass casualties on their enemies. These trends, in addition to the increasingly available expertise and technologies associated with nuclear fuel and weapons, have forced the international community to confront the global stockpile of fissionable material as a security priority. Given that HEU itself is scattered throughout the world in many forms and in a variety of different facility types, the global community faces a daunting challenge to secure, consolidate, and dispose of this material.

HEU Threat Assessment: Inventories and Incidents[14]

The world's existing stockpiles of HEU contain enough material to fabricate tens of thousands of additional nuclear weapons beyond the approximately 32,000 nuclear warheads that currently exist. Reliable estimates of the global HEU stockpile do not exist. Much of the existing HEU material is associated with military programs, and much of that material exists in fabricated warheads. Moreover, the rates of production and disposition in many countries

---

[13] For further reading, see, for example, Committee on International Security and Arms Control, *Management and Disposition of Excess Weapons Plutonium*, National Academy Press, Washington, DC, 1994; Cirincione, Joseph, et al., *Deadly Arsenals: Tracking Weapons of Mass Destruction*, Brookings Institution Press, Washington, DC, 2002; Bunn, Matthew, Anthony Wier, and John P. Holdren, *Controlling Nuclear Warheads and Materials: A Report Card and Action Plan. Project on Managing the Atom*, Harvard University (commissioned by the Nuclear Threat Initiative), March 2003.

[14] To begin the process of addressing the threat from HEU terrorism, we propose to start with a quantity of material significantly less than the global inventory of HEU (current estimates are in the range of 1,600 metric tons, plus or minus up to 30 percent). Nor do we propose to start with the approximately 60 metric tons of HEU associated with the full category of research reactors. Rather, we propose to begin with a subset of research reactors that are found in regions that are of current concern, whether they be located in developing nations or in regions of current instability. The near-term goal of addressing the most vulnerable material first, therefore, is a much more finite problem.

are not openly shared, even with the International Atomic Energy Agency. That the world is awash in HEU is not entirely accurate; nonetheless, sufficient material exists, in insufficiently secured locations, to warrant urgent national security concerns.

Both from the standpoint of a terrorist bent on either mass destruction or mass disruption and from the perspective of a state that has chosen to pursue a nuclear weapons program, the possibility of acquiring HEU is a tempting venture. The properties of weapons-grade HEU,[15] as opposed to plutonium, for example, make it desirable for bomb makers. Weapons-grade HEU poses less of a radiation problem for handlers, and it therefore makes the material relatively easy to work with in comparison to plutonium. Designs for explosives packages are well known and widely available, and proliferators would probably not feel the need to test such a device. The material's minimal heat production and its difficulty to detect make it relatively easy to steal.

The IAEA sets standards of accounting accuracy for fissile material. For HEU, a significant quantity is deemed to be 25 kilograms. However, a bomb maker would need approximately 50 kilograms of HEU to produce a gun-type weapon, or approximately 15 kilograms to produce an implosion-type weapon. The number of incidents of illicit trafficking in nuclear materials has steadily grown in recent years. Data tracked by the member states of the IAEA indicate that interest in fissionable materials from criminal actors remains intense. Table 2[16] shows the number of known incidents of illicit nuclear trafficking from 1993 to 2000, and Table 3 gives some examples of confirmed incidents of theft involving HEU.

---

[15] Enriched to at least 90 percent U-235.
[16] The nuclear material referred to here includes HEU, plutonium, LEU, natural uranium, and so forth.

	1993	1994	1995	1996	1997	1998	1999	2000	2001	2002	2003	Total
Nuclear Material	33	44	23	17	15	8	8	12	11	8	3	**182**
Other Radioactive Material	22	23	18	8	14	24	31	37	37	35	51	**300**
Both Nuclear and Other Radioactive Material	0	2	1	0	0	3	6	2	6	2	1	**23**
Radioactively Contaminated Material	1	0	0	1	3	3	7	5	3	4	3	**30**
Other	0	0	1	0	0	0	1	0	0	1	2	**5**
Total	**56**	**69**	**43**	**26**	**32**	**38**	**53**	**56**	**57**	**50**	**60**	**540**

Table 2 –Incidents of Illicit Nuclear Trafficking. Source: International Atomic Energy Agency, Illicit Trafficking Database by participating Member States, as of 20 July 2004. *Source: http://www.iaea.org/NewsCenter/Features/RadSources/chart1.html.*

More significant, the incidents specifically involving HEU indicate a nascent market for the material. Fortunately, there are no reported cases of trafficking in amounts significant enough to construct a device. This, however, does not mean that buyers and sellers are dormant, or that they will not eventually connect.

Date	Location	Material Involved	Incident Description
May 24, 1993	Vilnius, Lithuania	HEU: 150 grams	4.4 tons of beryllium, including 140 kilograms contaminated with HEU, were discovered in the storage area of a bank. Beryllium was imported legally.
March, 1994	St. Petersburg, Russia	HEU: 2.972 kilograms	An individual was arrested in possession of HEU, which he had previously stolen from a nuclear facility for sale.
June 13, 1994	Landshut, Germany	HEU: 0.795 grams	A group of individuals were arrested in illegal possession of HEU
December 14, 1994	Prague, Czech Republic	HEU: 2.73 kilograms	HEU was seized by police in Prague.
June 1, 1995	Moscow, Russia	HEU/ 1.7 kilograms	An individual was arrested in possession of HEU, which he had previously stolen from a nuclear facility.
June 6, 1995	Prague, Czech Republic	HEU: 0.415 grams	An HEU sample was seized by police in Prague.
June 8, 1995	Ceske Budejovice, Czech Republic	HEU: 16.9 grams	An HEU sample was seized by police in Ceske Budejovice.
May 29, 1999	Rousse, Bulgaria	HEU: 10 grams	Customs officials arrested a man trying to smuggle HEU at the Rousse customs border checkpoint.
April 19, 2000	Batumi, Georgia	HEU: 770 grams	Four individuals were arrested in possession of HEU.
July 16, 2001	Paris, France	HEU: 0.5 grams	Three individuals trafficking in HEU were arrested in Paris. The perpetrators were seeking buyers for the material.

Table 3 – Examples of Confirmed Incidents of Theft Involving HEU. Source: International Atomic Energy Agency, Illicit Trafficking Database by participating Member States, as of 20 July 2004. Source: _http://www.iaea.org/NewsCenter/Features/RadSources/table1.html_.

IV. CTR Budgets[17]

From an initial allocation of $400 million made available for reprogramming from the Department of Defense Budget in 1992, CTR (including nuclear, chemical, and biological weapons) has expanded and grown to include average appropriations of approximately $1 billion annually, divided among the Departments of Defense, State, and Energy.[18] Between FY 1992 and FY 2004, roughly $12 billion has been allocated by Congress for all CTR programs in the former Soviet Union. The historical review of CTR-related budgets is provided here as background to the scope of work required for a global application of the program.

A breakdown of this funding by U.S. federal agency is shown in Chart 1.[19] Charts 2 and 3 provide funding for Nuclear Warhead and Materials Control by U.S. federal agency and by programmatic goals. All charts use current dollars.

---

[17] Any analysis of a program such as CTR necessarily requires judgments as to what program elements to include and how aspects of the program should be categorized. For example, American observers usually include the U.S.–Russian HEU Purchase Agreement under the broader heading of Nunn–Lugar, whereas Russians often choose to consider that program a commercial venture outside of the more traditional donor-client relationship embodied in Nunn–Lugar. We haven taken a maximalist view and have included all programs that relate to weapons of mass destruction threat-reduction cooperation. We have also categorized individual program elements differently than other analytical reports and databases to more readily draw anecdotal information for CTR expansion. Therefore, aggregated numbers within the categories listed in this report may differ from those of our colleagues.

[18] The original Nunn–Lugar funding provisions for FY 1992 (PL 102-229) provided DOD with the authority to transfer up to $400 million of its existing budget; it did not provide new or additional money to the CTR program. The funding provisions for FY 1993 (PL 102-396) provided DOD with an additional $400 million in transfer authority. During these early years of the program, DOD and the FSU governments spent their time establishing the necessary legal instruments, building support, and designing the program. Therefore, DOD did not have large or expensive projects available to use the full transfer authorities in those years. Moreover, the types of monies that were made available for transfer within DOD were from a variety of different account types (procurement, operations and maintenance, construction, research and development) and therefore had a corresponding number of different use rules. Most important, different types of money are available for use for differing lengths of time; for example, research and development money must be obligated the same fiscal year for which it was appropriated or it expires, whereas procurement money is typically available for three years. Starting in FY 1994, the Defense Appropriations Act (PL 103-139) provided approximately $400 million in direct budget authority. The FY 1994 legislation also extended through FY 1994 the time when up to $400 million could be transferred from other DOD accounts. Thus, the FY 1994 data show the $400 million in direct budget authority plus $192.8 million in transfers, or $592.8 million total. Of the $800 million in transfer authority between FY 1992 and FY 1994, the total used by DOD was $451.9 million ($12.8 million in FY 1992, $246.3 million in FY 1993, and $192.8 million in FY 1994).

[19] Data for these charts are courtesy of Anthony Wier, Project on Managing the Atom, Belfer Center for Science and International Affairs, John F. Kennedy School of Government, Harvard University.
Note: this data does not include the State Department's Nonproliferation and Disarmament Fund, which has contributed to the general and specific goals enumerated here. The authors of this report have adjusted the Harvard data to conform to the analysis herein; judgments or errors are the sole responsibility of the authors.

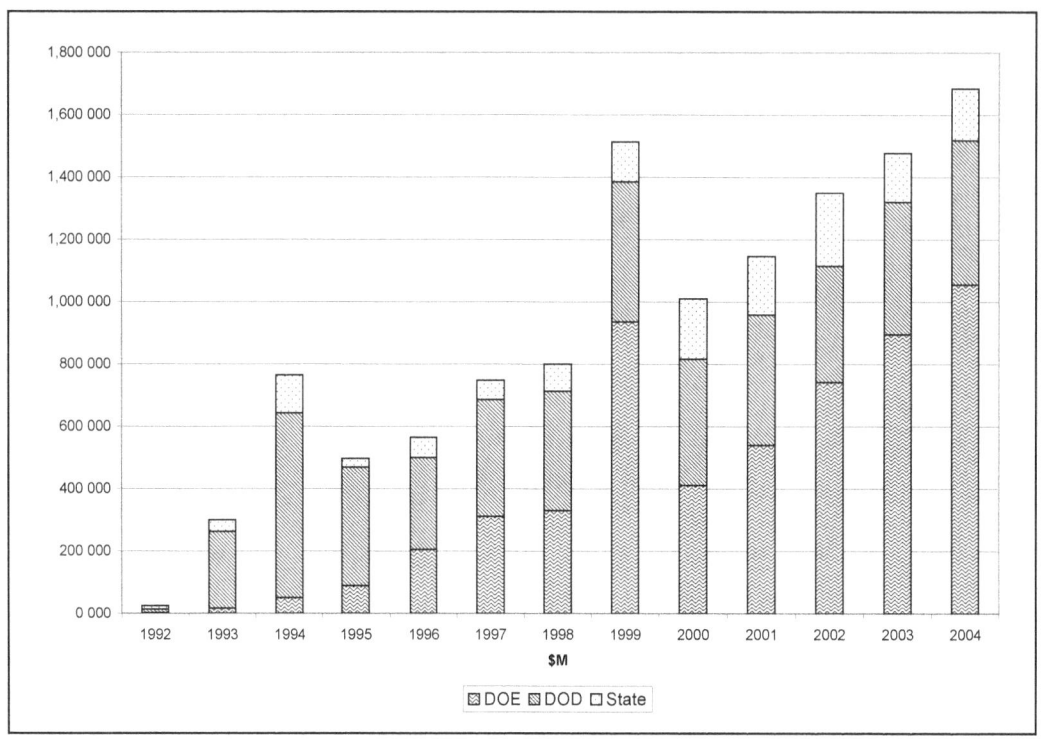

Chart 1 – Funding by Agency

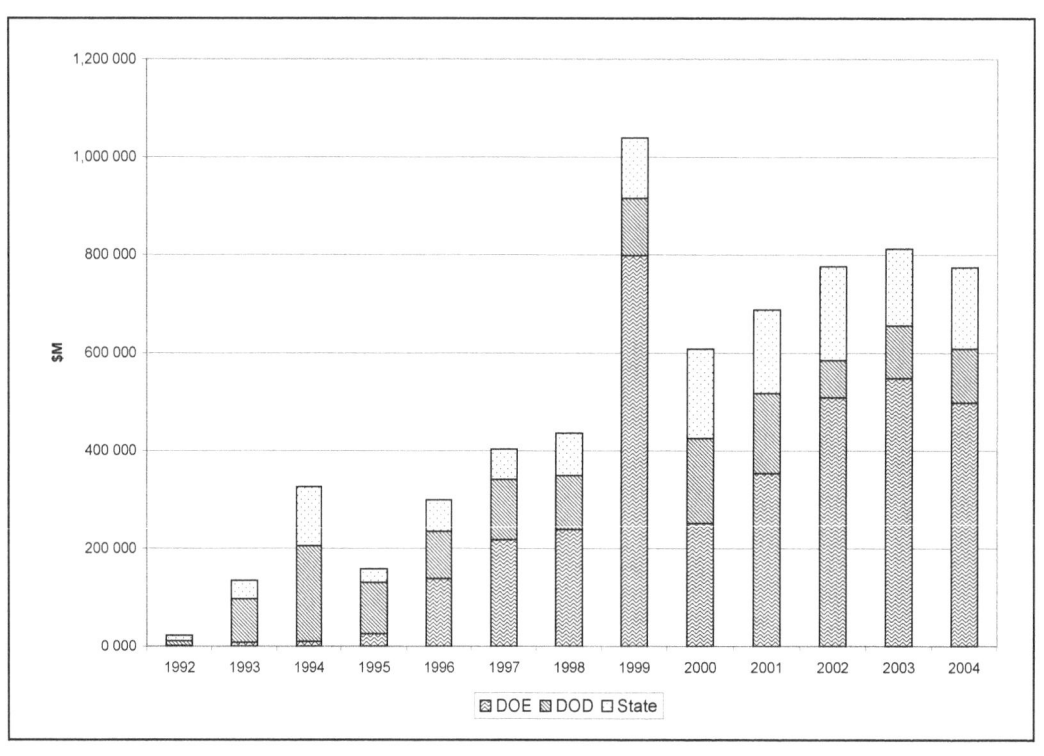

Chart 2 – CTR Nuclear Warhead & Materials Control Funding by Agency

14

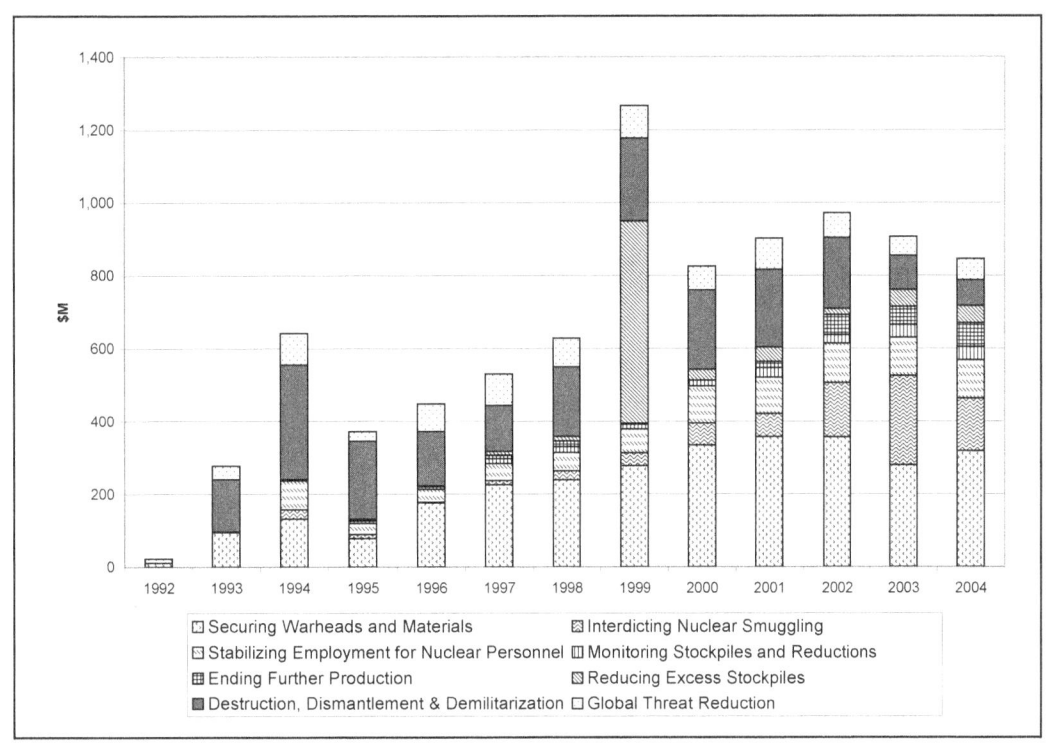

Chart 3 – CTR Nuclear Warhead & Materials Control Funding by Goals

As a general rule, CTR has enjoyed aggregate funding allocations from Congress for nuclear programs at or above the levels requested by the president on an annual basis. On 27 June 2002, the Group of Eight (G8) leaders established the Global Partnership Against Weapons and Materials of Mass Destruction (commonly referred to as the Global Partnership) at their summit in Kananaskis, Canada. Under the Global Partnership, the U.S. committed to providing approximately $1 billion per year over 10 years, whereas the other G8 partners committed to an additional $10 billion, for a total commitment of $20 billion. This initiative essentially captured the existing U.S. CTR budget at the time. Senior policy makers noted that funding for any new initiatives, either within the existing Russia programs or globally, would not lead to funding over the $1 billion annual target, and therefore, would require decrements to existing projects.[20]

However, there does appear to be some political will for funding increases. Overall budgets have steadily increased throughout the program, particularly for the DOE programs.

---

[20] Thornton, Charles, "The G8 Global Partnership Against the Spread of Weapons and Materials of Mass Destruction" *The Nonproliferation Review*, Fall–Winter 2002, Volume 9, Number 3, pp. 135–152.

The budget peaked in FY 2004 at $1.7 billion, and the president has requested roughly the same amount, $1.6 billion, for FY 2005.

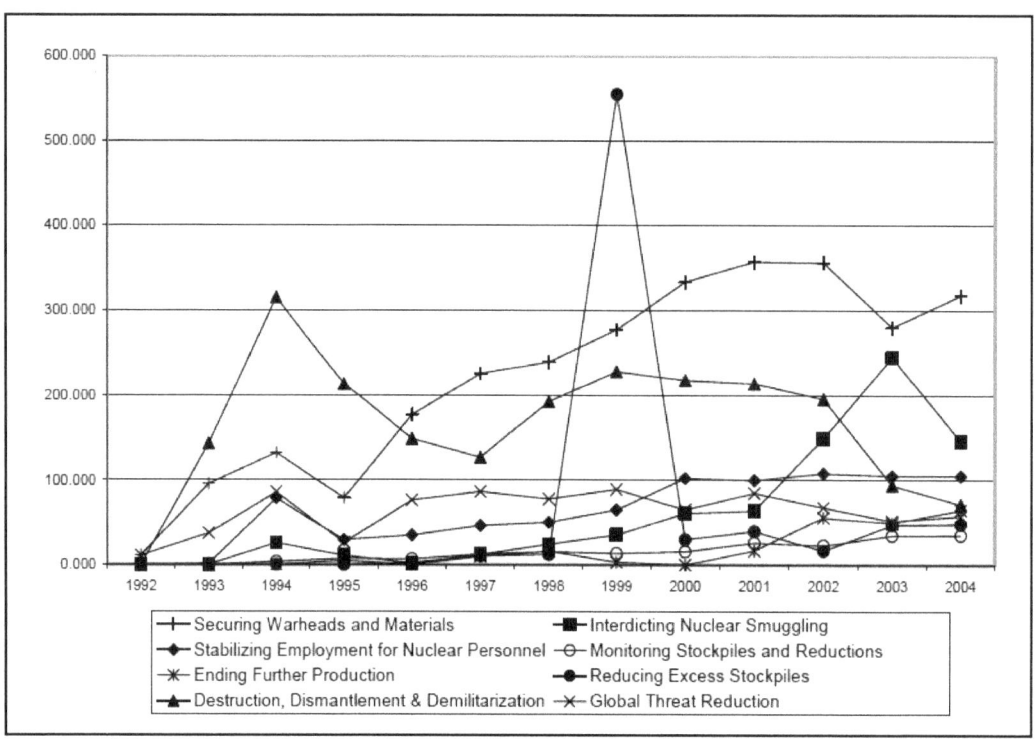

Chart 4 – Trends in CTR Nuclear Warhead & Materials Control Funding

It is clear from these trend lines where CTR policy has focused.[21] The highest priority of the DOD's element of the CTR program has remained the dismantlement of strategic delivery systems in the former Soviet Union. The Destruction, Dismantlement, and Demilitarization category has retained the most consistent funding level of all nuclear-related programs. Increasingly, though, Securing Warheads and Materials has enjoyed growing funding levels. This is for several reasons. First, the dismantlement programs were easier to implement because of their support of START implementation, whereas no analogous legal instrument has facilitated implementation of the nonproliferation-related projects. Second, U.S. and Russian policy makers, bureaucrats, and technical experts required more time to define the warhead and material security problems that needed to be addressed, in no small

---

[21] Note: The spike in DOE's FY 1999 budget was the result of one-time budgets for Reducing Excess Stockpiles in Russia. Specifically, Congress appropriated $230 million for Russian plutonium disposition and $325 million for the HEU Purchase Agreement.

part because of the continuing secrecy surrounding those activities in both countries. Third, the provision of security enhancements, and particularly first phases of quick-fix equipment, was relatively inexpensive compared to the massive undertaking required for dismantling a missile, submarine, or aircraft. And fourth, all sides have steadily increased the urgency with which they view the proliferation threats associated with the nuclear warheads and materials.

Some expert observers continue to believe that major new CTR initiatives would not receive new financing and, therefore, need to be funded out of the existing budgets. However, recent high-level attention from the president and the secretary of energy, as well as steadily increasing budget trends, indicate that new sources of financial support may be made available. The new initiatives recommended by this report will require substantial funding increases to address the unfinished business of CTR. However, because it will take some time to establish the international working relationships necessary to begin implementing these proposals, and as reprogramming authority for existing unobligated funds exists in the short term at the departmental levels, necessary funding increases may be phased in over time.

V. Priority Tasks for CTR in Russia and Obstacles Hindering Their Completion

Category 1—Russia

The Nunn–Lugar program was a bulwark against the acquisition of nuclear weapons by rogue states and terrorist organizations after the collapse of the Soviet Union. It was decisive in denuclearizing Belarus, Kazakhstan, and Ukraine. It helped Russia dismantle and eliminate nuclear weapons systems in accordance with the timetable laid out in the START I treaty. Yet much still remains to be done. The most critical of those unfinished tasks, according to Senator Lugar's own list, include the following:[22]

- Tactical nuclear weapons elimination and secure storage;
- Extending the MPC&A programs in Russia;
- Shutdown of plutonium-producing reactors;
- Fabricating plutonium into mixed oxide (MOX) fuel to be used in commercial reactors; and
- Converting reactors that use HEU to lower-enriched fuels and safely storing spent fuel.

In the nuclear field, Senator Lugar also lists American corporate investment into or purchase of Russian laboratories, eliminating widespread use of radioactive generators, and the dismantling of nonstrategic submarines.

A report written by Matthew Bunn and Anthony Wier for the Nuclear Threat Initiative (NTI), whose chair is former Senator Nunn, also lists several priorities.[23] These include:

---

[22] Senator Richard G. Lugar, "Nunn–Lugar Cooperative Threat Reduction: Senator Dick Lugar's Top Ten," < http://lugar.senate.gov/nunnlugar html>, accessed on 16 June 2004.

[23] Matthew Bunn, Anthony Wier, John P. Holdren, *Controlling Nuclear Warheads and Materials, A Report Card and Action Plan*, JFK School of Government, Harvard University, March 2003.

- Securing the most vulnerable nuclear sites around the world, in Russia and elsewhere, in many cases by removing nuclear material to safe locations;

- Accelerating a partnership with Russia to ensure that all of its nuclear weapons and materials are effectively secured and accounted for as rapidly as possible;

- Securing, monitoring, and dismantling the most dangerous warheads, particularly those that are easily portable and not equipped with modern versions of electronic locks;

- Expanding and reforming efforts to interdict nuclear smuggling;

- Stabilizing employment for nuclear personnel; and

- Reducing nuclear stockpiles and putting effective monitoring and data exchanges in place for these materials.

There is naturally some overlap between Senator Lugar's list and the NTI list. A consolidated list of priorities is presented in Table 4 below. The following tasks are the authors' priorities in Russia and are numbered according to their urgency.[24]

1. Reducing the number of sites where HEU is located and accelerating the blend down of HEU
2. Extending and tightening control over nuclear weapons and materials
3. Interdicting nuclear smuggling
4. Securing and dismantling those warheads that may be more portable (tactical nuclear weapons)
5. Safely disposing of existing plutonium and ending future production of weapons-grade plutonium
6. Reducing nuclear weapons stockpiles and putting monitoring and data exchanges in place

Table 4 – Priority Tasks for Nunn–Lugar CTR Programs in Russia

---

[24] We have omitted the question of supporting technical personnel in the former Soviet Union because we think that issue should move into the sphere of private enterprise.

Reducing the Number of Sites Where HEU is Located. Although the DOE MPC&A Program in Russia has been arguably one of the most successful Nunn–Lugar programs in Russia, much more still needs to be done. Russia has hundreds of tons of HEU scattered throughout the country. Many of the stockpiles are improperly secured and lack adequate material accounting systems. The problem here is one of priority. A policy decision to assign this task the higher priority it deserves is necessary to secure more resources.

Extending Control. The shortage of resources in comparison with the magnitude of the problem has been documented in several studies, but at this time, resources are not the major impediment in Russia. The main problem is a lack of commitment to the objectives of Nunn–Lugar in Russia, compounded by suspicions regarding U.S. intentions, and an ability to overcome problems related to taxation and liabilities. These problems are in need of serious high-level attention by both the U.S. and Russian governments. Conflicting priorities are limiting progress. For example, some actions taken by the United States are heightening the salience of nuclear weapons in Russia, thus affecting CTR implementation. Another area in need of immediate attention relates to continuing security issues at Russian nuclear facilities. The lack of adequate security and material accounting systems, coupled with growing terror threats to facilities housing nuclear weapons and materials, necessitates an acceleration of U.S. and Russian efforts to address this threat.

Interdicting Nuclear Smuggling. Cooperation has been fairly good between the United States, Russia, and the former Soviet states, but it has broken down in two respects. First, there have been instances in which Russian enterprises have exported nuclear related equipment, allegedly without export permits. In addition, a lack of resources has hampered the installation of equipment at ports and border crossings that could detect illicit goods. To be fair, this applies to the United States as well as the former Soviet Union.

Securing and Dismantling Tactical Nuclear Weapons. Russian tactical nuclear weapons are among the most dangerous from a terrorist perspective because they are small and, therefore, may be more easily portable; because they are designed for use with widely available conventional delivery systems; and because they lack sophisticated security devices that would reliably prevent unauthorized use. They are not covered by any formal arms control treaty, and voluntary measures announced in the early 1990s by the United States and Russia have lacked transparent and consistent implementation. Tactical nuclear weapons are a very sensitive issue for the Russians. With the restructuring of U.S. forces in Western Europe, an opportunity may arise to accede to a long-standing Russian proposal that all tactical nuclear weapons should be located within the national territories of their owners. This proposal should be linked to the bilateral mechanisms established by the 2002 Treaty of Moscow, so that limitations, reductions, and some form of mutual monitoring of adherence could be negotiated within that framework.

Safely Disposing of Plutonium and Stopping Production of Weapons-Grade Material. The key to this problem is lack of monetary resources, but differing views on the issue also play a role. Concern over liability issues stemming from an accident at a United States–funded and government- or industry-built weapons disposition or dismantlement site further compounds the problem. A number of American experts posit that it would be preferable to have weapons-grade plutonium embedded in vitreous logs and thus rendered unusable. Russians believe that plutonium can serve a useful purpose as fuel for reactors. It has been agreed that a pilot project would be launched to dispose of existing Russian plutonium. However, disposition of plutonium by fabricating it into MOX fuel will require extensive costs for the construction of the required facilities. Neither the United States nor Russia wants to foot the bill to replace them. A possible alternative for the MOX pilot plant that should be examined is the use of thorium fuel for nuclear power. Thorium-based nuclear fuels would leave far less waste plutonium than conventional fuels, and the plutonium that is created is unsuitable for use in bombs.[25]

Reducing Nuclear Weapons and Putting Monitoring and Data Exchanges in Place. The Senate imposed a condition on its consent to ratification of the 2002 Treaty of Moscow, which requires the administration to provide estimates of the numbers of deployed warheads. Little progress has been made thus far to implement this requirement.

The methods and technologies for dealing with these six tasks are well known; however, ingenuity is needed to overcome the obstacles technology alone can not address. Ingenuity is necessary both in adopting tried and true techniques to new tasks and in taking advantage of advances in technology. The main obstacles that must be overcome include

---

[25] Mujid S. Kazimi, *American Scientist Online*, "Thorium Fuel for Nuclear Energy," September–October 2003, Volume 91, Number 5 <http://www.americanscientist.org/template/AssetDetail/assetid/25710?fulltext=true>.

slow Russian implementation, lack of incentives, conflicting national security requirements, conflicting policy priorities, and management problems.[26] The problems that these conditions create differ from case to case, but one or more of them apply in varying degrees to each of the six priority tasks identified in Table 4.

Overcoming the Obstacles

A review of the obstacles confronting those who would like to deal with these priority tasks in Russia shows that in half the cases more progress can be made, and no major policy differences stand in the way. These priority tasks include:

- Extending controls over nonmilitary sites where weapons-useable material is located;
- Interdicting nuclear smuggling; and
- Reducing the number of sites where HEU is stored.

Two other priority tasks involve military considerations that will be difficult to resolve, absent a joint presidential-level decision. Specifically:

- Securing and dismantling tactical nuclear weapons; and
- Reducing nuclear weapons stockpiles and putting monitoring and data exchanges in place.

In general, concerns in Russia may continue to hinder U.S. efforts to help tighten controls over sites within the Russian military complex. Only a high-level political commitment in the two countries that this is worth doing will overcome the differences and resistance.

Another candidate for broader scope of cooperation is the accelerated elimination of large unnecessary stocks of Russian weapons materials, especially HEU. Depending on how

---

[26] For more information on this subject, see the National Research Council of the National Academies *"Report of a Joint Workshop: Overcoming Impediments to U.S.-Russian Cooperation on Nuclear Nonproliferation,"* 2004, <http://www.americanscientist.org/template/AssetDetail/assetid/25710?fulltext=true>.

stockpile reductions are implemented, they can drastically reduce the costs of security upgrades and maintenance, and of course, material that does not exist cannot be stolen and used.

With regard to CTR funding, there has been a general complaint from opponents of the program in the United States that American funding of such programs in Russia allows the Russians to avoid expending their own capital on these projects, freeing up money to be spent on other areas of national interest. Two recent events indicate that there may be some change in Russian attitudes. First, Russia has recently committed to providing $2 billion dollars over the next 10 years as part of the G8 Global Partnership Against Weapons and Materials of Mass Destruction initiative. Second, in the wake of recent terrorist bombings associated with the war in Chechnya, the Russians appear to be taking more seriously the threat posed by terrorists gaining access to nuclear material, especially when such materials are located within their own borders. Nonetheless, the program should be reviewed to insure that it includes the right incentive structure for Russia.

Sufficient funding, personnel, and organizational resources must be made available for these projects by both the United States and Russia. Congress should provide the funding during those fiscal years that is required for efficient implementation, and enough government and contractor personnel need to be available to both manage and execute the projects. Careful structuring of such programs and incentives will allow for both oversight and control. Incentives can be structured in such a way as to reward the rapid removal and destruction of weapons and materials while penalizing efforts that fail to achieve the desired results. Key here is the continued use of an effective verification regime based on the experience of CTR and other programs. By tying funding to results achieved, many of the bureaucratic obstacles that are still encountered can be overcome.

A comprehensive review of the Nunn–Lugar program in Russia determining where the bottlenecks are and what must be done to remove them should be conducted jointly by Russia and the United States. A U.S.–Russia summit meeting could then revitalize the program, as well as solidify commitments to follow through on obligations.

VI. Applying CTR Techniques in de facto Nuclear Weapon States

Category 2—India and Pakistan

India

India's nuclear weapons program originated in the mid-1940s with the inauguration of the Tata Institute of Fundamental Research in Bangalore. The Department of Atomic Energy was created in 1954, when Indian Prime Minister Jawaharlal Nehru launched a dual-use, three-stage nuclear program.[27] The first stage of the nuclear power program was aimed at exploiting the abundant natural thorium reserves in the country, and in 1955 the first thorium plant went into production in Trombay. Although the initial goal of the nuclear program was to focus on the production of inexpensive electricity, the decision to develop a complete nuclear fuel cycle led to the technical capability to build nuclear weapons, and a nuclear explosives program was begun in 1968.[28] This program progressed quickly, with uranium-233 separated from irradiated thorium in 1970 and underground testing of a fission device taking place on 18 May 1974.[29] Advances by neighboring rival Pakistan in the late 1980s in the development of a nuclear weapons capacity spurred Indian Prime Minster Rajiv Gandhi to authorize the weaponization of India's nuclear capability.

By May 1994, Indian scientists had developed the capability to deliver nuclear weapons using combat aircraft, and by 1996 they had developed a nuclear warhead for the Prithvi-1 ballistic missile.[30] In 1998, India successfully carried out two rounds of underground nuclear tests, and the country formally declared itself a nuclear power. The first round of testing took place on 11 May 1998, when the country carried out three underground tests at their Pokhran range, and two more underground tests were held on 13 May 1998.[31] There is considerable debate over the yield and reliability of India's nuclear devices.

---

[27] Gaurav Kampani, "India Profile: Nuclear Overview," Nuclear Threat Initiative
<http://www.nti.org/e_research/profiles/India/Nuclear/index html>, accessed on 21 September 2004.
[28] Ibid.
[29] Ibid.
[30] Gaurav Kampani, "India Profile: Nuclear Overview," Nuclear Threat Initiative
<http://www.nti.org/e_research/profiles/India/Nuclear/index html>, accessed on 21 September 2004.
[31] Federation of American Scientists, "India: Nuclear Weapons,"
<http://www.fas.org/nuke/guide/india/nuke/index.html>, accessed on 21 September 2004.

India has 14 operating nuclear power reactors, mostly heavy-water moderated and natural-uranium fueled. It has 12 more under construction, including two of the VVER Russian-designed light-water, low-enriched uranium (LEU) reactors. It has one breeder reactor in operation and another under construction. Of its eight research reactors, four have now been dismantled or decommissioned. It has two pilot ultracentrifuge plants for the production of enriched uranium and two laser enrichment research activities. Three reprocessing plants are operating (one on a laboratory scale and another large-scale plant is under construction). Six uranium processing operations are underway. Ten heavy-water production plants have been built, and all but one is still operating. [32] Estimates credit India with enough separated plutonium to fabricate anywhere between 40 and 120 nuclear weapons. [33]

India's missile program, indigenously developed, includes the liquid-fueled Prithvi, with ranges from 150 to 350 kilometers and a payload of 500 kilograms or more. The newer, solid-fueled Agni II has a range of up to 2,500 kilometers and a 1,000-kilogram payload. [34] India is planning a longer-range version of that missile. Although its missile program is quite active, India relies mainly on air-delivered weapons and probably will continue to do so for some time.

The objectives of the United States regarding India's nuclear program are quite different from those discussed with regard to Russia. India represents the second category of nuclear threat reduction mentioned at the beginning of this report: nuclear weapons programs in de facto nuclear weapon states. Five important goals in which a Nunn–Lugar approach could be helpful include:

1. Ensure that India acts as though it were a member of the Nuclear Nonproliferation Treaty (NPT) as regards transfers of weapons, materials, and technology;
2. Help India maintain its nuclear establishments in conditions that are safe and secure and in which leakage of weapons, materials, and technology will not occur;

---

[32] Joseph Cirincione et al., *Deadly Arsenals: Tracking Weapons of Mass Destruction*, Carnegie Endowment for International Peace, 2002.
[33] Gaurav Kampani, "India Profile: Nuclear Overview," Nuclear Threat Initiative <http://www.nti.org/e_research/profiles/India/Nuclear/index html>, accessed 21 September 2004.
[34] Ibid.

3. Encourage India to avoid a regional nuclear arms race by capping its nuclear forces at a low level and not conducting further nuclear weapons tests;

4. Promote a stable Indo-Pakistan nuclear relationship through the types of measures envisaged in the Lahore Declaration and avoiding a posture based on rapid launch procedures; and

5. Encourage India to join in regional and global nuclear arms restraint regimes.

It should be recognized at the outset that progress toward achieving these goals will require U.S. diplomacy of the utmost delicacy and will also require a defense relationship that promotes trust and confidence between India and the United States. It will also require an effort that is carefully orchestrated, if only informally, with India's neighbors: China, Pakistan, and Russia. In fact, it may be desirable to encourage another nation to take the lead in dealing with India; Canada or France might be candidate countries, but it is essential that India accepts the objectives of a Nunn–Lugar type program if Pakistan is to be induced to accept them as well.

Even in this complex situation, a Nunn–Lugar approach could make a contribution. Several CTR tools could be adapted from the experience in the former Soviet Union and applied in the case of India.

APPLYING CTR TOOLS IN THE CASE OF INDIA

1. **Improving physical control of items of interest.** Partnering organizations and states can provide the training and know-how for authorized access, personnel, and reliability security checks, automated inventory control and management systems, and site security enhancements, including electronic surveillance and control systems and perimeter barriers and fences around Indian sites. Improving physical control of items of interest will be a key tool that can be used during the disarmament process to safeguard the Indian facilities and materials of greatest concern.

2. **Improving accountability for items of interest.** On the basis of the Russian experience, procedures for the improved accountability of nuclear materials have been developed that can be employed in other countries as well. These include the use of audits by inspection teams to ensure the continued and proper use of these measures and integrated inventory systems to enhance India's ability to account for and track materials. These tools are very important because of the enormous size and diversity of India's nuclear weapons program.

3. **Preventing the leakage of technology to unauthorized recipients.** This refers to helping weapons scientists to find gainful employment in civil jobs and also to controlling how information is shared. Programs and information exchange should be developed that will help experts make the transition to civilian work and employment. Indian scientists and engineers are among the best trained in the world and will need to make the transition in the civilian sector. Laboratory-to-laboratory exchanges, research grants and programs, and employment in civilian energy products are methods that can be used.

4. **Preventing the export of nuclear weapons, materials, and equipment.** To ensure that nuclear weapons and related materials and equipment are not diverted to other proliferating states and terror organizations, programs aimed at establishing verifiable safeguards and increasing transparency and national export controls to prevent illicit smuggling of nuclear weapons/components need to be developed.

New methods may be useful that do not arise directly from experiences with Nunn–Lugar in the former Soviet Union but, rather, from U.S. experience with the Soviet Union and with the management of the U.S. weapons stockpile. These could include Nuclear Risk Reduction Centers or shared early warning. Some argue that such cooperation might be inconsistent with the NPT, which is why it would be important to secure Indian and Pakistani commitments to act in accordance with NPT restrictions on transfer of weapons and materials and, if possible, to negotiate a Fissile Material Cutoff Treaty. According to Rose Gottemoeller and Rebecca Longsworth in a Carnegie Endowment for International Peace working paper, there may be aspects of the NPT regime and the Nuclear Suppliers Group that India and Pakistan would be willing to adopt as their own policy: "It may be possible, therefore, to encourage these countries to develop new cooperation with the regime and at the same time establish joint projects to enhance physical protection of nuclear materials."[35] Key to success will be for India and Pakistan to start with small pilot projects, experiments, and exchanges of best practices and then work into larger cooperation as confidence in these efforts builds.

Pakistan

For many years the United States has been concerned about Pakistan's nuclear weapons–related activities and about the continuing tension between Islamabad and neighboring India. Recent assassination attempts against Pakistani leader General Pervez Musharraf and the discovery of a covert nuclear materials black market involving Pakistani nuclear scientists further exacerbates American concerns over the stability of the country's nuclear weapons and materials. It would be in the best interest of both the United States and Pakistan to cooperate in securing Pakistan's nuclear weapons and related materials to safeguard against, for example, the illicit export of nuclear weapons, materials, and equipment.

Pakistan's nuclear power program is not as extensive as India's. Pakistan took the enriched uranium route to a nuclear weapon, unlike India, which based its weapons program on plutonium. Pakistan's nuclear program was established in 1972 by Zulfiqar Ali Bhutto

---

[35] Rose Gottemoeller and Rebecca Longsworth, *Enhancing Nuclear Security in the Counter-Terrorism Struggle: India and Pakistan as a New Region for Cooperation.* Carnegie Endowment for International Peace, Working Paper Number 29, August 2002.

after the country lost the Indo-Bangladesh war of 1971.[36] After India's underground testing of a nuclear device in 1974, Pakistan acquired sensitive uranium enrichment technology and expertise in the late 1970s with the arrival Dr. Abdul Qadeer Khan, a German-trained metallurgist. Dr. Khan brought with him the knowledge of gas centrifuge technology and, reportedly, stolen blueprints for uranium enrichment technologies from the Netherlands.[37] Under Khan's direction, Pakistan employed an extensive clandestine smuggling network to obtain the materials and key technologies required for uranium enrichment capabilities.

By the mid-1980s, Pakistan had developed a uranium enrichment facility, and experts believe that by 1986 the country had produced enough weapons-grade uranium for the production of its first nuclear weapon. The Khan Research Laboratory is where A. Q. Khan's famous ultracentrifuge facility is located and where weapons-grade uranium is fabricated into weapons. A heavy-water, natural uranium power reactor and two light-water, LEU power reactors make up Pakistan's entire inventory of such reactors. Pakistan has several centers for uranium processing, including mining, milling, and conversion into uranium fluoride. There are also two facilities for production of heavy water.[38]

Pakistan's ballistic missile program is also well developed, with assistance from China and North Korea, and is considered superior to that of India's. The Ghauri missile is based on North Korea's No Dong liquid-fueled missile. It has a 1,300-kilometer range and can carry a payload of 850 kilograms. The Shaheen I missile, based on Chinese technology, is a solid-fueled, 750-kilometer range missile with, perhaps, a 500-kilogram payload.[39] All these missiles could reach important targets in India while carrying nuclear weapons.

On 28 May 1998, in response to nuclear weapons tests by India, Pakistan announced that it had successfully conducted five nuclear tests. Pakistan declared itself a nuclear power and conducted one more test on May 30 in Chagai Hills in the western part of the country. In February 2000, Pakistan established a Nuclear Command Authority and consolidated the Khan Research Laboratories and the Pakistan Atomic Research Corporation into the Nuclear

---

[36] Federation of American Scientists, "Pakistan Nuclear Weapons,"
<http://www.fas.org/nuke/guide/pakistan/nuke/index html>, accessed on 21 September 2004.
[37] Ibid.
[38] Joseph Cirincione et al., *Deadly Arsenals: Tracking Weapons of Mass Destruction*, Carnegie Endowment for International Peace, 2002.
[39] Ibid.

Defense Complex.[40] Some of the key Pakistani nuclear facilities include the Karachi Nuclear Power Plant, the Khusab 50-MWt heavy-water and natural uranium research reactor, the Nuclear Defense Complex, the Pakistan Institute of Nuclear Science and Technology, and Sihala, which is reportedly the site of a non-safeguarded pilot-scale uranium enrichment plant. Pakistan is thought to have enough weapons-grade uranium for between 30 and 50 nuclear weapons.[41]

American strategic objectives with regard to Pakistan are focused mainly on helping Pakistan fight terrorism. Another major concern is maintaining political stability in a highly volatile country, where radical Islamists hold a position of considerable strength. The danger of another Indo-Pakistan war over Kashmir seems to have receded, but the possibility can never be discounted. Finally, in late 2003 and early 2004, it came to light that Dr. Khan, the "Father" of Pakistan's nuclear weapons program, had disseminated nuclear weapons–related technologies, equipment, and know-how to Iran, North Korea, and Libya. This may be the most pressing danger stemming from the Pakistani program and a development that must never be permitted to happen again.

As with the case of India, competing U.S. goals (e.g., stability in Pakistan, cooperation in the fight against terrorism) limit what the United States can do to promote nonproliferation and nuclear restraint in the region or globally. As with India, it might be better for another country, such as China, to take the lead in this effort. There are a number of tools relating to the CTR program that can be applied to Pakistan. Specifically, six tools used in the former Soviet Union might be applied.

---

[40] Federation of American Scientists. "Pakistan Nuclear Weapons: A Brief History of Pakistan's Nuclear Program" <http://www.fas.org/nuke/guide/pakistan/nuke/>, accessed 21 September 2004.
[41] Joseph Cirincione et al., *Deadly Arsenals: Tracking Weapons of Mass Destruction*, Carnegie Endowment for International Peace, 2002.

APPLYING CTR TOOLS IN THE CASE OF PAKISTAN

1. **Improving physical control of items of interest.** Partnering organizations and states can provide the training and know-how for authorized access, personnel, and reliability security checks and automated inventory control and management systems. Vulnerability assessments should be done on each facility, and security at weapons storage sites needs to be ensured, including adding video and radio surveillance equipment, perimeter barriers, and fences. Given the current instability in Pakistan, and the recent assassination attempts on President Musharraf, improving physical control of items of interest will be a key tool that can be used during the disarmament process to safeguard Pakistani facilities and the materials of greatest concern.

2. **Improving accountability for items of interest.** On the basis of the Russian experience, procedures for the improved accountability of nuclear materials have been developed that can be employed in other countries as well. These include the use of audits by inspection teams to ensure the continued and proper use of these measures. Each facility should have computerized databases and tracking systems to account for nuclear weapons, materials, and related technologies. These tools are very important because of recent discoveries of illicit transfer of sensitive nuclear technologies from Pakistani scientists to third parties.

3. **Preventing the leakage of technology to unauthorized recipients.** This refers to helping weapons scientists to find gainful employment in civil jobs and also to controlling how information is shared. Programs and information exchange should be developed that will help experts make the transition to civilian work and employment. Laboratory-to-laboratory exchanges, research grants and programs, and employment in civilian energy products are methods that can be used.

4. **Preventing the export of nuclear weapons, materials, and equipment.** To ensure that nuclear weapons and related materials and equipment are not diverted to other proliferating states and terror organizations, programs aimed at establishing verifiable safeguards and increasing transparency and national export controls to prevent illicit smuggling of nuclear weapons/components need to be developed. Knowledge of the vast nuclear black market program in which high-ranking Pakistani nuclear scientists were involved increases the urgency of and necessitates the need for verifiable safeguards and interdiction programs in Pakistan.

5. **Hardening transportation links against attack.** Nuclear weapons and materials could be vulnerable while being transported from one point to another. Protection for weapons in transit can be provided under this tool by employing such techniques as railcar safety enhancements, training of security personnel to protect transportation routes, and the provision of supercontainers to secure fissile materials in transit.

6. **Purchasing HEU for resale as fuel for commercial nuclear power plants.** Techniques used in the former Soviet Union regarding the purchase of HEU can be applied to Pakistan's nuclear weapons program. To reduce the threat of diversion, theft, or sale of Pakistan's HEU, the United States could implement a U.S.–Pakistan Highly Enriched Uranium Purchase Agreement, whereby HEU from dismantled Pakistani weapons is blended down to LEU, and thus becomes less of a proliferation threat. Pakistan can apply the funds the United States provides for the sale of HEU to securing its nuclear weapons program.

Providing security enhancements for Pakistan's nuclear warheads will be a tricky endeavor. In the case of Russia, the United States has restricted nuclear warhead security assistance to those projects that can demonstrate direct support to the dismantlement effort. In the case of Pakistan, there is no dismantlement program. The program would focus on promoting stability and enhancing deterrence. Nonetheless, there are certain projects that may enhance warhead security while minimizing enhancements to military capabilities.

As mentioned above, in the case of India, other methods derived from U.S. experience outside the CTR context might also be useful and should be explored within the context of an Indian and Pakistani commitment to the broad purpose of the NPT. Both India and Pakistan, for example, might be more likely to participate in Nunn–Lugar-type projects that are multilateral in approach, and they should be encouraged to participate in both regional and global projects. Furthermore, both India and Pakistan should consider expanding joint discussions of accidental/unauthorized launch to include first responders as a way to clarify the devastating effects of actual nuclear use, or the panic effects of rumors or threats.

VII. Applying CTR Techniques in the Cases of Former Noncooperative States

Category 3—Libya

For more than 30 years, the U.S.–Libyan bilateral relationship was marked by intense suspicion and hostility. U.S. policy toward Libya focused on Libya's sponsorship of terrorism and its pursuit of weapons of mass destruction. In 1979, the United States designated Libya as a state sponsor of terrorism, and in 1986, it imposed comprehensive, unilateral sanctions on all commercial and financial transactions with the other country.[42]

The turning point in American–Libyan relations occurred at the end of 2003 with Libya's renouncement of its illicit weapons of mass destruction program and its vow of openness with international inspectors. Increasing openness and engagement by Libya has allowed international participation in dismantling Libya's weapons program and demonstrates how Nunn–Lugar CTR tools can be used in the case of a former rogue state. Even though it ratified the NPT on 26 May 1975, in the mid- to late 1970s, Libyan leader Muammar al-Qadhafi publicly expressed interest in acquiring nuclear weapons capability. Soliciting outside assistance, Libya made a first attempt to acquire nuclear technology from China that was rebuffed, but in 1979, Libya received a 10-MW nuclear research reactor from the Soviet Union and installed it at a research center at Aura, near Tripoli.[43] Libya reached an agreement with the IAEA in 1980 to place all of Libya's nuclear installations under international inspection authority; however, the country still continued to work with the Soviet Union. In the mid-1980s, Libya obtained a commitment from Moscow for the construction of an 880-MW power station to be located in the Surt region.[44] When the United Nations sanctions were lifted from Libya in 1998, Russia renewed its nuclear cooperation, providing funding for renovations to the Tajura nuclear complex.

---

[42] Neumann, Ronald. "U.S. Policy Towards Libya," 30 November 1999
<http://www.fas.org/news/libya/991130_neumann_libya htm>.
[43] Federation of American Scientists, "Libya Special Weapons"
<http://www.fas.org/nuke/guide/libya/index.html> accessed 21 September 2004.
[44] Nuclear Threat Initiative, "Libya Overview," January 2004
<http://www.nti.org/e_research/profiles/Libya/index html>.

Following months of secret negotiation with the United States and the United Kingdom, on 19 December 2003, Libya announced that it would dismantle its weapons of mass destruction and ballistic missile programs. This was linked to a Proliferation Security Initiative (PSI) success in interdicting a shipment of centrifuge equipment. Libya informed the IAEA that for over a decade it had been engaged in the development of a uranium enrichment capability, including importation of uranium, centrifuge, and conversion equipment. During the 1980s, the country conducted undeclared laboratory and bench-scale uranium conversion experiments at Tajura, and with the help of a foreign expert, Libya initiated a research and development program on uranium gas centrifuge enrichment.[45] However, it had extremely limited indigenous capabilities, and Libya stated that no industrial-scale facility had been built.

Libya declared 12 sites that had been involved in its covert nuclear program since the 1980s and agreed to an Additional Protocol to its NPT Safeguards Agreement, giving the IAEA full access to its nuclear weapons program. An IAEA inspection team determined that the nuclear weapons program was in the early stages and was three to seven years away from producing a nuclear weapon.[46]

On 22 January 2004, nuclear weapons design information from Libya was sent to the United States, and on 26 January 2004, U.S. officials airlifted about 55,000 pounds of nuclear-related materials to the United States. In March, an additional 1,000 tons of centrifuge parts and MTCR-class missile parts were shipped out of the country. As a result of the existing sanctions on Libya and the fact that it is on the U.S. state sponsor of terrorism list, the U.S. Administration is currently using the State Department's Nonproliferation and Disarmament Fund to help disarm Libya because it is ineligible for CTR aid.[47]

The United States and the IAEA are already using a number of nonproliferation tools to dismantle Libya's weapons of mass destruction program. These tools include dismantling and removing nuclear weapons components, fissile materials, and equipment for producing weapons-usable fissile material from the country, as well as removing the means of

---

[45] IAEA, "Implementation of the NPT Safeguards Agreement of the Socialist People's Libyan Arab Jamahiriya," GOV/2004/12, 20 February 2004.
[46] IAEA, "Implementation of the NPT Safeguards Agreement of the Socialist People's Libyan Arab Jamahiriya," GOV/2004/12, 20 February 2004.
[47] Sharon A. Squassoni and Andrew Feickert, *Disarming Libya: Weapons of Mass Destruction*, CRS Report for Congress, 22 April 2004.

delivering nuclear weapons and for diverting technical and scientific expertise to civil purposes. The dismantlement of Libya's weapons program demonstrates how Nunn–Lugar CTR tools can be used in the case of a former rogue state.

APPLYING CTR TOOLS IN THE CASE OF LIBYA

1. **Diverting technical and scientific expertise to civil purposes**. Since the program was initiated in the 1970s, many hundreds of Libyan scientists and experts have been trained in nuclear research and development. These scientists and engineers should be trained to have their knowledge diverted to useful civilian purposes, including indigenous energy supply development. Scientist-to-scientist and laboratory-to-laboratory exchanges and cooperative agreements will offer Libyan weapons experts new research topics in civilian areas and help eliminate the threat of future weapons proliferation.

2. **Preventing the export of nuclear weapons, materials, and equipment**: Programs and information exchange should be developed that will help experts make the transition to civilian work and employment and will encourage them to not transfer their scientific know-how to third parties. To ensure that nuclear weapons and related materials and equipment are not diverted from Libya to other proliferating states and terror organizations, programs aimed at establishing verifiable safeguards and increasing transparency and national export controls to prevent illicit smuggling of nuclear weapons/components need to be developed.

3. **Assisting in the conversion of defense industries or weapons laboratories to civil operations.** The aim of this tool is to convert parts of the Libyan nuclear weapons complex to civilian purposes through identifying and developing nonmilitary applications for them. Libyan research and development centers can be converted for use in peaceful purposes, including the Tajura research center. Using private funds, as well as public funds, this approach has also sought to convert weapons centers to business enterprises.

VIII. Considering CTR Techniques in the Cases of Noncooperative Proliferators

Category 4—North Korea and Iran

Preventing the spread of nuclear weapons technologies, materials, and expertise is one of the highest national and international priorities for the United States. On 11 February 2004, at a speech at the National Defense University in Washington, DC, President George Bush recognized the openness of Libya in renouncing its weapons of mass destruction program and encouraged North Korea and Iran to follow Libya's example. Iran is pursuing a nuclear weapons capability and North Korea probably has such a capability. Nonetheless, it is useful to identify the techniques that might be available should these states agree to cooperate. In fact, identifying these techniques in advance may be useful to U.S. and allied negotiations as they seek to terminate these programs.

North Korea

North Korea first began its nuclear program in 1952 with the establishment of the Atomic Energy Research Institute and the Academy of Sciences, which form the institutional base for the country's covert nuclear weapons program. In 1956, the North Koreans established cooperative nuclear agreements with the Soviet Union, allowing them to send scientists and teachers to the USSR for training.[48] In the early 1960s, the Soviet Union provided a variety of technical assistance while North Korea constructed the Yŏngbyŏn Nuclear Research Center, supplying a Soviet IRT-2000 Nuclear Research Reactor to the facility, which became fully operational in 1967.[49]

By 1974, North Korea managed to independently expand the IRT-2000 reactor, using indigenous technology. At the same time, scientists began work on building a 5-MW(e) graphite-moderated natural uranium reactor. Operational in 1986, the 5-MW(e) plant has irradiated an estimated 8,000 fuel rods. A plant for the chemical extraction of plutonium from

---

[48] Nuclear Threat Initiative, "North Korea Profile: Nuclear Overview" <http://www.nti.org/e_research/profiles/NK/Nuclear/index.html>, accessed 21 September 2004.
[49] Ibid.

spent fuel rods is also situated near Yŏngbyŏn and has evidently extracted weapons-useable plutonium.

By the mid-1980s, North Korea had begun construction on a 50-MW(e) nuclear power reactor at the Yŏngbyŏn Nuclear Complex, ostensibly for the production of electricity.[50] In 1985, North Korea acceded to the NPT but refused to sign a nuclear safeguards agreement with the IAEA until April 1992.

In 1994, the country accepted the U.S.–DPRK Agreed Framework, whereby North Korea agreed to freeze its nuclear program and halt the construction of a 200-MW(e) power reactor at Taechon and the 50-MW(e) nuclear power plant. In return, the United States agreed to lead an international consortium to construct two light-water power reactors and provide 500,000 tons of heavy fuel oil per year until the first reactor came online with a target date of 2003.[51] Subsequently, however, intelligence revealed that North Korea had begun to acquire a uranium enrichment capacity. With that discovery, the Agreed Framework quickly fell apart.

On 10 January 2003, North Korea notified the IAEA that it was withdrawing from the NPT and that it would restart its nuclear reactors. On 23 April 2003, at roundtable discussions in Beijing, a North Korean diplomat reportedly stated that North Korea possessed nuclear weapons.[52] North Korea probably has fabricated two to three nuclear devices (some estimates place this number as high as six to eight), but it is not known where these are stored or where the weapons fabrication center is located.

North Korea has participated in ongoing "six-party" negotiations with China, Japan, South Korea, Russia, and the United States that are aimed at dismantling its nuclear weapons program. North Korea has stated that it must receive a "reward" for taking the preliminary steps toward a nuclear freeze. During negotiations in June 2004, the United States presented an offer of energy and security guarantees in exchange for North Korea dismantling its program. North Korea's proposal reportedly would freeze its main nuclear facility at Yŏngbyŏn in exchange for energy/fuel aid, removal from the U.S. list of state sponsors of terrorism, and an end to economic sanctions. Its proposal, however, would not address North

---

[50] Nuclear Threat Initiative, "North Korea Profile: Nuclear Overview" <http://www.nti.org/e_research/profiles/NK/Nuclear/index.html>, accessed 21 September 2004.
[51] Federation of American Scientists, "North Korea: Nuclear Weapons Program" <http://www.fas.org/nuke/guide/dprk/nuke/index html>, accessed 21 September 2004.
[52] Ibid.

Korea's HEU efforts. In early July 2004, National Security Advisor Condoleeza Rice stated that North Korea could reap "surprise" rewards if it dismantled its nuclear weapons program. Continued negotiations, however, have yet to result in any agreement between North Korea and the United States.

North Korea is also a major producer of ballistic missiles, based on Soviet "Scud" technology. Facilities for production and testing of the 1,000-kilometer-range No Dong missile are located at Hwaedae-Gun. The missile is capable of carrying a payload of up to 1,000 kilograms. It is likely that the long-range Taepo Dong missile is fabricated there as well. North Korea is working on a Taepo Dong II missile with a range capable of striking the continental United States.[53] Nuclear weapons research centers are located in and around Yŏngbyŏn and in Pyongyang. In total, there are probably several hundred professional-level scientists and engineers associated with the fissile material production centers and with ballistic missile research, development, and production.

Without reference to the dynamics of the negotiating process or its final outcome, it is clear that there are six key tasks that need to be addressed for North Korean disarmament: freezing all plutonium and uranium production, dismantling all facilities relevant to the manufacture and production of nuclear weapons, eliminating any nuclear weapons, dismantling or converting ballistic missile production facilities, eliminating ballistic missiles, and preventing illicit export or transfer of fissile materials, nuclear weapons, weapons-relevant technology, and the means of delivery (this would be a meaningful objective in the interval between a freeze and total dismantlement of nuclear and missile facilities). Because North Korea is on the State Department's sponsor-of-terrorism list and is therefore currently ineligible for CTR aid, it would be useful to begin discussions with America's partners in the "six-party" talks regarding how the application of CTR techniques could be managed and funded in North Korea.

Several of the CTR methods identified in Table 1 for dealing with North Korea's nuclear facilities could be deployed to address these key areas.

---

[53] Joseph Cirincione et al., *Deadly Arsenals: Tracking Weapons of Mass Destruction*, Carnegie Endowment for International Peace, 2002.

APPLYING CTR TOOLS IN THE CASE OF NORTH KOREA

1. **Improving physical control of items of interest.** The IAEA and other partnering organizations and states can provide authorized access, personnel and reliability security checks, automated inventory control and management systems, and site security enhancements, including cameras, fences, and sensors. As well, North Korean scientists and technicians can engage in exchange of technical information related to nuclear weapons safety and security. Improving physical control of items of interest will be a key tool that can be used during the disarmament process to safeguard some of North Korea's weapons-dedicated facilities, including the Yŏngbyŏn Nuclear Complex, which houses a number of research and development centers, as well as nuclear fuel rod production plant, the 5-MW(e) experimental reactor, and the IRT-2000 reactor. In Russia, key technologies and approaches used to secure nuclear warheads and materials included rapid security upgrades, including bricking over windows and installing monitoring and security detectors at doors and other key points of weapons facilities.

2. **Improving accountability for items of interest.** On the basis of the Russian experience, procedures for the improved accountability of nuclear materials have been developed that can be employed in other countries as well. These include the use of audits by inspection teams to ensure the continued and proper use of these measures and computer tracking/accounting systems to improve the accounting of nuclear weapons.

3. **Diverting technical and scientific expertise to civil purposes.** North Korea's nuclear weapons program spans the complete nuclear fuel cycle. Thousands of North Korean scientists and experts have been trained in nuclear research and development. These scientists and engineers can be trained to have their knowledge diverted to useful civilian purposes, including indigenous energy supply development. Scientist-to-scientist and laboratory-to-laboratory exchanges and cooperative agreements will offer North Korean weapons experts new research topics in civilian areas.

4. **Preventing the leakage of technology to unauthorized recipients.** This refers to helping weapons scientists find gainful employment in civil jobs and also to controlling how information is shared. Programs and information exchange should be developed that will help experts make the transition to civilian work and employment and to encourage them to not transfer their scientific know-how to third parties.

5. **Preventing the export of nuclear weapons, materials, and equipment.** To ensure that nuclear weapons and related materials and equipment are not diverted to other proliferating states and terror organizations, programs aimed at establishing verifiable safeguards and increasing transparency and national export controls to prevent illicit smuggling of nuclear weapons/components need to be developed.

6. **Eliminating means of delivering nuclear weapons.** Under the START I treaty and the Lisbon Protocol, Nunn–Lugar funds were used to physically destroy launchers, missiles, and bombers. In North Korea, such funds can be used to disable, transport, and store strategic nuclear delivery vehicles and facilities. These funds can also be used to build service roads for access to missile silos, for incinerators to destroy liquid rocket fuel and oxidizer, and for cranes to help prepare missile silos for dismantlement and destruction.

7. **Assisting in the conversion of defense industries or weapons laboratories to civil operations.** The aim of this tool is to convert parts of the North Korean nuclear weapons complex to civilian purposes through identifying and developing nonmilitary applications for these components. Many of the research and development centers in North Korea can be converted for use for peaceful purposes. Using private funds as well as public funds, this approach has also sought to convert weapons centers to business enterprises.

8. **Supporting alternative power sources.** Under the Agreed Framework in 1994, North Korea agreed to freeze activity of its 5-MW(e) reactor in exchange for two light-water power reactors. Construction of both reactors has yet to be completed. Alternative conventionally fueled power plants could be constructed with external support.

9. **Removing nuclear weapons, fissile materials, and equipment for producing weapons-useable fissile material from countries of concern.** To safeguard the nuclear weapons and fissile material and related equipment associated with North Korea's weapons program, the country could agree to the removal of weapons, material, and related equipment capable of producing weapons-useable fissile material to safe storage in Russia or other participating countries, pending final disposition.

40

Iran

The Shah first initiated Iran's nuclear research program in the 1950s. Progress was slow until the late 1960s, when a U.S.-supplied 5-MW thermal research reactor went online at the Tehran Nuclear Research Center.[54] Iran signed the NPT in 1968. Iran concluded several contracts for the construction of nuclear plants and the supply of nuclear fuel; however, the nuclear program was slowed with the advent of the Islamic Revolution in 1979, when Ayatollah Khomeini came to power. Further, a number of structures were damaged by Iraqi bombings during the Iran–Iraq war. The program did not gain momentum again until 1984.

In the mid-1980s, Iran began laboratory experiments involving the production of heavy water, and in 1990 Iran began negotiations with the Soviet Union over completion of the Bushehr reactors and the supply of additional nuclear plants. In January 1995, the Russian Federation formally announced that it would complete the construction of the Bushehr reactors and signed an agreement with Iran for two light-water, LEU reactors.[55] These are the "proliferation-resistant" type of reactors that the United States supported in the case of North Korea as replacements for older, graphite-moderated reactors. Russia has asked that the spent fuel rods be returned to Russia for reprocessing, so that Iran would not have access to weapons-useable plutonium. At the moment, neither reactor is in operation.

In 2003 Iran acknowledged that it had engaged in illicit activities under the NPT Safeguards Agreement. Investigations into the disclosures by the IAEA have found that Iran's nuclear program consisted of a nearly complete front end of a nuclear fuel cycle, including uranium mining and milling; fuel fabrication; heavy-water production; a light-water reactor; and a heavy-water research reactor. Iran has also acknowledged the separation of small amounts of plutonium.[56] The disclosure by Iran in 2003 that it failed to report activity that was illicit under the NPT Safeguards Agreement has led to serious concern in the international community over the country's nuclear weapons program.

---

[54] Nuclear Threat Initiative, "Iran Profile Nuclear Overview," December 2003 <http://www.nti.org/e_research/profiles/Iran/1819.html>.
[55] Ibid.
[56]IAEA, "Implementation of the NPT Safeguards Agreement in the Islamic Public of Iran," GOV/2003/74, 10 November 2003, < http://www.fas.org/nuke/guide/iran/nuke/iaea1103.pdf>.

In February 2003, the Iranian government acknowledged that it was constructing two centrifuge enrichment plants. The foreign ministers of Britain, France, and Germany secured an agreement from the government of Iran that it would suspend the building of its gas centrifuge facility at Natanz. It is not clear that this commitment has been fulfilled in all respects. In addition, in August 2003, environmental samples taken by IAEA inspectors at the Kalaye Electric Company revealed the presence of HEU particles and LEU particles that were not consistent with the nuclear materials in Iran's inventory.[57]

Iran's ballistic missile program has profited from North Korean support. Iran has 100 Scud-Cs and the capacity to manufacture more. It hopes to produce the No Dong missile in a model called the Shahab III, which also uses Russian SS-4 MRBM technology, supplied by Russian companies. Tests to date have not been particularly successful.[58] Iran is developing a longer-range version called the Shahab IV, which would have a range of 2,000 kilometers and a payload of 1,000 kilograms. The government also has announced plans for a Shahab V, with a range that might be in the vicinity of 6,000 kilometers.[59]

In December 2003, Iran signed an Additional Protocol to its NPT Safeguards Agreement, giving IAEA inspectors the right to make intrusive, immediate inspections of Iranian facilities. However, Iran continues to be uncooperative with IAEA inspectors and claims that it is trying to establish a complete nuclear fuel cycle to support a civilian energy program, although it is widely believed that the country's efforts are focused on uranium enrichment.[60] There are also some indications that Iran is conducting work on plutonium production. Iran has stated that it plans to build a heavy-water facility for research; however, once completed, the nuclear reactor could be capable of producing weapons-grade plutonium. On 19 June 2004, the IAEA published a report stating that Iran had yet to ratify the IAEA Additional Protocol, and that verification of whether or not Iran had suspended its uranium enrichment program had been delayed because of the continued production of

---

[57] IAEA, "Implementation of the NPT Safeguards Agreement in the Islamic Public of Iran," GOV/2003/74, 10 November 2003, < http://www.fas.org/nuke/guide/iran/nuke/iaea1103.pdf>.
[58] Joseph Cirincione et al., Deadly *Arsenals: Tracking Weapons of Mass Destruction*, Carnegie Endowment for International Peace, 2002.
[59] Ibid.
[60] For more information on strategies to prevent Iran from proliferating, please see Brent Scrowcroft, "U.S. should define strategy to keep Iran from making nuclear weapons," Salt Lake Tribune, <http://166.70.46.216/2004/Jun/06252004/commenta/178721.asp>, accessed on 21 September 2004.

centrifuge equipment.[61] Furthering international concern, in late June 2004, Iran stated that it would restart the production of uranium centrifuge parts assembly and testing.

The U.S. position is that neither the Bushehr reactors nor the Natanz gas centrifuge plant are necessary because Iran has abundant sources of energy. The clearest policy that the administration has expressed regarding issues such as these is in the president's National Defense University speech on 11 February 2004. In it, President Bush assured nations that they would receive nuclear fuel so that they need not reprocess fuel rods for plutonium or enriched uranium. IAEA Director General Mohamed ElBaradei has spoken of multilateral facilities to preclude national bomb-making capabilities. Nunn–Lugar CTR techniques might be useful in promoting these ideas, although new ground will have to be broken to do so, as past experience is not entirely analogous.

The main tasks to be accomplished in Iran include dismantling the Natanz plant, ensuring that spent fuel rods from Bushehr are returned to Russia (this assumes that Russia will insist on this method of safeguarding spent fuel rods and that at least one Bushehr reactor will be put into operation), and freezing the development of the Shahab series of ballistic missiles. There are a number of Nunn–Lugar CTR techniques that can be applied to these three tasks. Because Iran is on the State Department's sponsor-of-terrorism list and is therefore ineligible for CTR aid, it would be useful to begin discussions with Britain, France, and Germany regarding the application and funding of CTR techniques in Iran. A list of techniques might include:

---

[61] IAEA, "Implementation of the NPT Safeguards Agreement in the Islamic Republic of Iran," GOV/2004/48, 18 June 2004. <http://www.iaea.org/Publications/Documents/Board/2004/gov2004-49.pdf>.

APPLYING CTR TOOLS IN THE CASE OF IRAN

1.   **Improving accountability for items of interest**. On the basis of the Russian experience, procedures for the improved accountability of nuclear materials have been developed that can be employed in other countries as well. These include the use of audits by inspection teams to ensure the continued and proper use of these measures, as well as computerized databases and computer tracking systems.

2.   **Diverting technical and scientific expertise to civil purposes.** Thousands of Iranian scientists and experts have been trained in nuclear research and development. These scientists and engineers can be trained to have their knowledge diverted to useful civilian purposes, including indigenous energy supply development. Scientist-to-scientist and laboratory-to-laboratory exchanges and cooperative agreements will offer Iranian weapons experts new research topics in civilian areas. The Tehran Nuclear Research Center located at the University of Tehran is Iran's primary open nuclear research facility and would be a good candidate for this program.

3.   **Preventing the leakage of technology to unauthorized recipients.** This refers to helping weapons scientists find gainful employment in civilian jobs and also to controlling how information is shared. Programs and information exchange should be developed that will help experts make the transition to civilian work and employment.

4.   **Preventing the export of nuclear weapons, materials, and equipment**. In the 2003 Patterns of Global Terrorism report, the United States listed Iran as one of the seven designated state sponsors of terrorism with the Islamic Revolutionary Guard and Ministry of Intelligence and Security personnel involved in planning and supporting terrorist acts. To ensure that nuclear weapons and related materials and equipment are not diverted to other proliferating states and terror organizations, programs aimed at establishing verifiable safeguards and increasing transparency and national export controls to prevent illicit smuggling of nuclear weapons and components need to be developed.

5.   **Removing nuclear weapons, fissile materials, and equipment for producing weapons-useable fissile material from countries of concern.** To safeguard the nuclear weapons and fissile material and related equipment associated with Iran's weapons program, the country can agree to the removal of weapons, material, and related equipment capable of producing weapons-useable fissile material to safe storage in participating countries. One possible method of implementing this would be guaranteeing fuel supplies in return for giving up independent means of producing enriched uranium.

IX. Sources of HEU and Global Threat Reduction – Category 5

Whereas categories 1–4 of CTR expansion described in the preceding sections are intended to address the particular issues associated with specific countries, category 5 looks at international efforts to halt the threat from HEU. A key ingredient of nuclear weapons, HEU is found in many forms throughout the world. Although efforts are underway to address these threats, a new sense of urgency should focus international efforts on the most dangerous material located in facilities and regions of greatest concern.

Most HEU is located in military-related facilities. Except for the special cases described below, this material should be considered secure in a relative sense. Although the total quantity of material found on the civil side is much smaller, it poses a much greater proliferation concern. The following list summarizes the various forms of HEU[62]:

- Military inventory: in weapons, in naval reactors, in the weapons or naval reactor pipeline, and in reserve;
- Transitional inventory: material that has been removed from weapons or other military sources and that may or may not have been declared excess to weapons requirements; and
- Civil inventory: used in power generation or research.

It is difficult to separate the estimates for the military and transitional inventories. Today's global stockpile of military HEU may be in the range of 500 metric tons, whereas the transitional inventory may be in the approximate range of 1,100 metric tons.[63] The vast majority of these stockpiles are located in the United States, Russia, and the other authorized nuclear weapon states. The current Nunn–Lugar program is providing site security

---

[62] Derived largely from William Walker and Frans Berkhout, *Fissile Material Stocks: Characteristics, Measures and Policy Options*, United Nations Institute for Disarmament Research, New York and Geneva, 1999.

[63] These estimates start from those provided by David Albright and Mark Gorwitz, "Tracking Civil Plutonium Inventories: End of 1999," *Plutonium Watch*, October 2000. It also attempts to account for ongoing blend-down and utilization in naval reactors, primarily in Russia.

enhancements to nuclear warhead and fissile material storage sites in Russia. Although considerable work remains to be accomplished, both sides are highly engaged on the issues.

Overview of the HEU Problem

As of 31 January 2004, there were 440 nuclear power plants in operation and 31 nuclear power plants under construction around the world.[64] In general, power reactors are relatively secure, operated safely, and use fuel that is difficult to use or convert into explosive material, and those that are located in non–nuclear weapon states are under IAEA safeguards. This is not to claim that there is no threat associated with power reactors; in fact, the security of the reactor facilities and of the reactor fuel must remain a high priority.

The category of nuclear reactors that pose a more immediate proliferation threat is that of those used for research. According to the IAEA, there are currently 274 research reactors in operation, plus another 7 under construction, with 9 planned in the future, 214 shut down, and 168 decommissioned.[65] Research reactors are used to provide a neutron source for a wide range of applications. They are generally not used for power generation, but they often require much higher uranium enrichment for fuel, with typical levels ranging from 20 percent to 93 percent U-235.

Many of these reactors are old, obsolete, inoperative, or in need of repair. In some cases, stocks of spent fuel are stored in an insecure manner. In other instances, spent fuel has been building up for years with few opportunities for disposal. Some of these reactors are still fueled with highly enriched uranium, a key ingredient for assembling a nuclear weapon.[66]

Calculating the probability of a terrorist attack with HEU is a difficult undertaking. Analysts have attempted to use complex mathematical and statistical models relying on unlikely event scenarios. The most definitive results of their research, which generally coincide with the assessments of terrorism and proliferation

---

[64] International Atomic Energy Agency, Power Reactor Information System, 20 July 2004 <http://www.iaea.org/programmes/a2/index html>.
[65] International Atomic Energy Agency, Research Reactor Database, 20 July 2004 <http://www.iaea.org/worldatom/rrdb/>. Reporting by member states to the IAEA on "shut down" and "decommissioned" is often lacking. Therefore, these figures should be considered approximates.
[66] International Atomic Energy Agency, Promoting the Safety and Security of Research Reactors <http://www.iaea.org/>, accessed 21 July 2004.

experts, indicate that although the probability of nuclear terrorism is low, it is clearly increasing. Complementary to this calculation is the assertion that the military, economic, and social consequences of a nuclear terrorist attack are both high and increasing. A variety of initiatives by states, international agencies, and nongovernmental organizations are already under way to address this problem, including UN Security Council Resolution 1540 and the Department of Energy's Global Threat Reduction Initiative. It is difficult to discern, however, any overarching strategy or a consensus prioritization of the problems.

Research Reactors

We propose to deal, as an initial focus, with a small subset of the HEU found in the civilian sector. Of the total number of research reactors in operation, shut down, or decommissioned, only a subset uses HEU as fuel. The proposed initiative regarding those HEU-fueled research reactors is further limited to those located in regions of concern. In the near term, efforts should be directed more at facilities in developing countries or countries in transition, and less at facilities in states that are better equipped to provide for safety and security requirements. Among the solutions is a proposal to return the nuclear fuel, whether it is spent or fresh, to the country of origin.

Policy Options to Address the HEU-Fueled Research Reactor Challenge

Specific cooperative measures to secure the HEU found in these research reactors include, first, securing the material in place. If the managers intend to continue using HEU to fuel the reactors, then it may be necessary to provide security enhancements for the reactor facility itself. The question then becomes, what is secure enough? For material as dangerous as HEU, facilities must be effectively secured against the kinds of outsider and insider threats that terrorists and criminals have already demonstrated that they are able to pose.[67] That means that each country in which such material is going to continue to exist must put in place—and effectively enforce—regulatory requirements that facilities with potential bomb material be able to protect against a specified "design basis threat" based on the magnitudes

_____

[67] Bunn and Wier, *Securing the Bomb*, pp. 14–15.

of attack that have already been demonstrated in countries around the world if they are to be allowed to continue to operate. Mere compliance with existing IAEA recommendations is not sufficient, as it is well known that facilities can comply with these recommendations while remaining dangerously insecure. In many cases, it will be necessary to begin with simple rapid upgrades, such as piling heavy blocks over material or putting it into difficult-to-penetrate steel cages. The major advantages of this approach are that:

- At least limited improvements can be made quickly, even for facilities unwilling to give up their HEU.
- The systems designed and tested between the U.S. and Russia could serve as a model.

The major disadvantages are that:

- It may take longer to implement than removing the target HEU.
- It may cost more than removing the target HEU, and costs will continue as long as the HEU remains present.
- It relies on the state in which the material is located to pay to operate and maintain the security system over time, and it relies on guards and other personnel at the facility to maintain high security standards and a strong "security culture," which is difficult to achieve.
- It does not address the dangers posed by threats beyond those the security system is designed to address, such as senior facility management deciding to sell off material, state failure or regional anarchy, disgruntled military units seizing the facility and its material, or insider or outsider attacks that are more capable than the security system is able to protect against.

The second policy option is securing HEU through the removal of materials from regions of concern to the source states.[68] There are currently some 12,850 spent fuel assemblies of U.S. origin still at research reactors outside of the United States. They are eligible to be returned to the United States as long as they are discharged before 13 May 2006. Perhaps more disturbing, there are 24,803 spent fuel assemblies originally enriched in

---

[68] This is in line with the "Global Cleanout" proposal advanced by, among others, Matthew Bunn, Anthony Wier, John P. Holdren, *Controlling Nuclear Warheads and Materials: A Report Card and Action Plan, Project on Managing the Atom*, Harvard University, Washington, DC, March 2003.

the former Soviet Union still at research reactors outside of Russia.[69] The IAEA, Russia, and the United States have begun shipping unirradiated Russian-supplied fuel back to Russia and will begin shipping irradiated HEU fuel back to Russia as soon as internal Russian legal procedures can be completed. Both fresh and spent fuel that is not currently in use in reactor operations should be immediately returned to the countries of origin. The United States has been returning fuel since the outset of its export programs, though, as discussed in the third proposal below, it has done so inconsistently. Russia has recently returned fuel from reactors in Bulgaria, Romania, and Yugoslavia, as well as the former Soviet republics of Kazakhstan and Georgia. To undertake an operation to remove fresh or spent fuel from a research reactor facility, all sides will need to consider a decision matrix. That is, material in storage is inherently more secure than material in transit. However, policy makers will need to weigh the costs and benefits of securing in place versus consolidation in the source country and to determine the short- versus long-term issues of securing in place versus consolidation in the source country. In the long run, returning the fuel to the country of origin will usually far outweigh any short-term benefits of security found in leaving the fuel on site. The major advantages of this approach are that:

- Dangerous material is removed from the region of concern.
- Consolidated material is more efficiently and affordably secured.

The major disadvantages are that:

- Management at many facilities is currently unwilling to give up the facility's HEU. Substantial incentives are likely to be required, which may increase cost significantly in some cases.
- The process of moving the material places the HEU in its most vulnerable state for a short period.
- Sites in some source countries to which the material might be transported (e.g., Russia) are also insecure.

Secretary of Energy Spencer Abraham has announced plans to return all unirradiated Soviet-supplied HEU to Russia by the end of 2005, all irradiated Soviet-supplied HEU to

---

[69] International Atomic Energy Agency, "IAEA Promotes Research Reactor Safety," Staff Report, 8 March 2004, available at <http://www.iaea.org/NewsCenter/Features/ResearchReactors/security20040308 html> as of 30 July 2004.

Russia by the end of 2009, and the vast majority of U.S.-supplied HEU to the United States within four to five years. To achieve these objectives will require fast, comprehensive, and flexible implementation of the Global Threat Reduction Initiative, with targeted incentives offered to each facility to convince it to give up its HEU.

The third option is converting the reactor to use LEU rather than HEU. It is conceivable that the use of HEU to fuel research reactors could be eliminated altogether. The process of removing lightly-irradiated fuel, or even fuel that has not been irradiated, is not a technically difficult process, and the reactors could be redesigned to use LEU. A recent U.S. Government Accountability Office (GAO) report highlighted the ongoing problems with the conversion programs administered by the United States and Russia. Fourteen of the 20 foreign research reactors that currently use U.S.-origin HEU fuel do not have plans to convert to LEU. According to Argonne National Laboratory officials, these reactors generally have a supply of HEU sufficient to last many years (in some cases for the life of the reactor) and either do not want to incur the additional cost of conversion or do not have the necessary funding. Three of the reactors are planning to convert to LEU, and three others currently plan to shut down (or, in the case of two reactors, convert to LEU fuel if they do not shut down). According to Argonne officials, seven Russian-supplied research reactors, all located outside Russia, could convert using LEU fuels that are currently available or are expected to become available within the next year. However, only one of the seven reactors, located in Ukraine, is scheduled to convert.[70] The process of HEU to LEU conversion has been under way since the 1970s in the Reduced Enrichment for Research and Test Reactors program. Unfortunately, many of the current projects are being implemented much too slowly. Efforts, for example, under the Reduced Enrichment for Research and Test Reactors program to convert the core from HEU to LEU fuel in the Romanian research reactor have been ongoing for over a decade.[71]

---

[70] United States Government Accountability Office, "Nuclear Nonproliferation: DOE Needs to Take Action to Further Reduce the Use of Weapons-Usable Uranium in Civilian Research Reactors," Report to the Chairman, Subcommittee on Emerging Threats and Capabilities, Committee on Armed Services, U.S. Senate, GAO-04-807, July 2004.

[71] Toma, C., M. Ciocanescu, R. Dobrin, and M. Parvan, "Progress Report on HEU-LEU Core Conversion of the Triga-14 MW Reactor From Inr-Pitesti," Institute for Nuclear Research (Romania), Papers Presented by ANL at the RERTR Meeting, 1997 <http://www.td.anl.gov/Programs/RERTR/Analysis97/CToma-abs.html> as of 30 July 2004.

This program often works in conjunction with the second proposal above. Although the program has generally been a success, implementation has been haphazard. The United States has converted some of the reactors it supplied, though some facilities have refused to participate. Reactors fueled by states other than the United States have not been converted at nearly the same rate. Likewise, some reactors have not converted because an alternative fuel has not been provided. Finally, fuel origin states, including the United States, have not consistently allowed for the return of the spent fuel, often forcing the research reactor facilities to store it on site.

The Way Forward

Addressing the threats associated with the global stockpile of HEU is a daunting task. The targets are dispersed throughout the world, and the threats are politically and technically challenging. New approaches to address the threats posed to the HEU-fueled research reactors are not necessary. The policy tools and technical capabilities exist, are in place, and are tested. The policy options are only a representative set, not an exhaustive taxonomy.

What is now needed is more focus and attention of the policy community and senior leadership. Although there is not yet solid evidence that enough HEU for a bomb has been stolen, anecdotal evidence of the terrorist threat is abundant. To address the threat, the United States and its partner countries must look at securing and consolidating the existing stocks of HEU found in the least secure sites located in the most vulnerable regions.

Measuring the effectiveness of these solutions must be based first and foremost on security. Enhancing the security of the stockpile, through whatever means available, should be a top priority. Second must be the rate of implementation, and here speed is a critical factor. At the end of the list of criteria for success should be cost. The cost of these programs must be subordinated to improving national security.

X. Expansion of Global Threat Reduction

The early efforts to stem the expected tide of nuclear weapons proliferation were global in scope: the Nuclear Weapons Test Ban Treaty, the NPT, and the creation of the IAEA. New conditions, arising from the collapse of the Soviet Union, led to the Nunn–Lugar CTR program, which was bilateral in nature and focused on Russia and the former Soviet states of Belarus, Kazakhstan, and Ukraine. Now, the advent of global terrorism, accompanied by international black markets in nuclear materials, has once again created the need for a global response. Several initiatives have been taken by the current administration to counter the threat of weapons of mass destruction: the PSI, UN Security Council Resolution 1540, the G8's Global Partnership, and the Global Threat Reduction Initiative. Most of these initiatives are still in the early stages of being realized; however, each of these programs could potentially be joined to strengthen the nonproliferation regime overall.

On 31 May 2003, at a speech given in Paris just before the 2003 G8 Summit, President Bush announced plans for the PSI. The PSI is a broad international partnership of countries that coordinate their actions to interdict shipments of weapons of mass destruction, their delivery systems, and related technologies and materials.[72] The PSI is not a formal institution or treaty, and it does not replace other national and international nonproliferation mechanisms. Instead, it reinforces and compliments existing nonproliferation treaties, export controls, and other related enforcement measures. PSI participants work together to build operational capabilities to interdict the shipment and transfer of WMD and related materials worldwide and have engaged in air, ground, and sea interdiction training exercises. The PSI is consistent with and supports UN Security Council Resolution 1540 and recent statements of the G8 Global Partnership calling for greater efforts to be focused on preventing the proliferation of WMD, their delivery systems, and related materials.

Another international nonproliferation effort that could be part of a cohesive nonproliferation strategy on a global basis is UN Security Council Resolution 1540. Adopted on 28 April 2004, resolution 1540 recognizes that preventing rogue states and terrorist groups from acquiring nuclear weapons and related materials deserves the highest international

---

[72] The White House, "Statement on Proliferation Security Initiative," 4 September 2003 <http://www.whitehouse.gov/news/releases/2003/09/20030904-10.html>.

priority. UN Security Council Resolution 1540 calls on all member states to establish domestic controls and adopt legislative measures to prevent illicit trafficking of weapons of mass destruction, means of delivery, and related materials and technologies. The resolution calls on member states to establish a committee for a period of no longer than two years to report on the implementation of the resolution. States are required to present a first report to that committee, no later than six months from the adoption of the resolution, on steps they have taken or intend to take in its implementation.[73]

UN Security Council Resolution 1540 is just one among a series of global nonproliferation initiatives seeking, by various means, to achieve similar goals. In 2003, the G8 (composed of Canada, France, Germany, Italy, Japan, United States, United Kingdom, and Russia) met in France and agreed on an initiative entitled the "Global Partnership Against the Spread of Weapons and Materials of Mass Destruction," (initially referred to as "10 plus 10 over 10"). The Global Partnership committed the G8 to provide up to $20 billion over 10 years to fund nonproliferation projects in Russia and other nations and to reinforce the global nonproliferation regime. The Global Partnership is largely focused on Russia, but it could be expanded to deal with the broader global issue of proliferation.

At the June 2004 Sea Island Summit, the G8 member counties affirmed their support for UN Security Council Resolution 1540 and called on all states to implement the resolution promptly and fully. The Global Partnership also announced a number of new initiatives aimed at reducing the risk of nuclear weapons proliferation and the acquisition of nuclear materials and technology by terrorists. The G8 countries stated that the Global Partnership would establish new export control measures to control sensitive nuclear items with proliferation potential and established a one-year moratorium on provision of nuclear enrichment and reprocessing technologies to states that did not already have the technology.

The Global Partnership also agreed to support projects to eliminate the use of highly enriched uranium fuel in research reactors worldwide, secure and remove fresh and spent HEU fuel, control and secure radiation sources, and strengthen export control and border security. Furthermore, they stated that they would pursue the retraining of Iraqi and Libyan

---

[73] United Nations Security Council, "Security Council Decides all States Shall Act to Prevent Proliferation of Weapons of Mass Destruction," 28 April 2004 <http://www.un.org/News/Press/docs/2004/sc8076.doc htm>.

scientists involved in past WMD programs and that seven new countries would join the partnership.[74] They stated:

> We reaffirm that we will address proliferation challenges worldwide. We will, for example, pursue the retraining of Iraqi and Libyan scientists involved in past WMD programs. We also support projects to eliminate over time the use of highly-enriched uranium fuel in research reactors worldwide, secure and remove fresh and spent HEU fuel, control and secure radiation sources, strengthen export control and border security, and reinforce biosecurity. We will use the Global Partnership to coordinate our efforts in these areas.[75]

Though some have questioned the seriousness of this commitment, the fact that such an effort has even come into existence is a positive sign that world leaders recognize the seriousness of the threat posed by the uncontrolled spread of nuclear weapons, materials, and technology.

On 26 May 2004, in recognition that one of the most serious threats to American security is from the possibility of an attack with nuclear and radiological materials, Secretary of Energy Spencer Abraham announced the Global Threat Reduction Initiative (GTRI). According to Bill Hoehn of RANSAC:

> There has been no single, integrated U.S. government program, with a defined budget and resources, for facilitating a systematic clean-out of vulnerable nuclear material storage facilities around the world, though the Department of Energy (DOE) is now in the process of trying to improve coordination of various key activities under a single umbrella of its proposed Global Threat Reduction Initiative.[76]

GTRI, thus, is not a new DOE program but, rather, is a consolidation of authority from several existing programs with emphasis on securing or removing high-risk nuclear and radiological materials and equipment in countries around the world, to prevent them from falling into the hands of rogue states or terror organizations.[77] As Secretary Abraham states:

---

[74] G8 "Action Plan on Nonproliferation," June 2004 <http://www.g8usa.gov/d_060904d.htm>.
[75] Ibid.
[76] Personal communication with Bill Hoehn, RANSAC, July 2004.
[77] Department of Energy, "Global Threat Reduction Initiative Highlights" <http://www.energy.gov/engine/doe/files/dynamic/264200491138_Vienna_GTR_Fact%20Sheet_FINAL1_052 604%20.pdf>.

This Global Threat Reduction Initiative is an attempt to present a workable strategy for addressing the threat posed by the entire spectrum of nuclear materials. It reflects the realities of the 21st century that were so startlingly made clear on a September morning three years ago. We have developed this initiative with the expectation it can comprehensively and more thoroughly address the challenges posed by nuclear and radiological materials and related equipment that require attention, anywhere in the world, by ensuring they will not fall into the hands of those with evil intentions. We will do this by the securing, removing, relocating or disposing of these materials and equipment—whatever the most appropriate circumstance may be—as quickly and expeditiously as possible.[78]

According to Secretary Abraham, $450 million will be used for repatriating all Russian-origin, HEU fuel by the end of 2005 and accelerating the repatriation of all Russian-origin spent fuel by 2010; accelerating repatriation of U.S.-origin spent fuel; converting the cores of civilian research reactors that use HEU to use LEU instead; and identifying other nuclear and radiological materials and related equipment that are not yet covered by existing threat reduction efforts.[79] The new initiative will establish a new office under the Deputy Administrator for Defense Nuclear Nonproliferation, a Global Materials Recovery Team, and a global database to identify and prioritize nuclear materials and equipment of proliferation concern.

President Bush, in his 11 February 2004 speech at the National Defense University, outlined a series of measures designed to prevent the proliferation of nuclear weapons.[80] Several of these have relevance to the Nunn–Lugar CTR program and could be addressed by an extension of the CTR concept. Specifically, President Bush proposed seven new steps to help combat the development and spread of weapons of mass destruction. The seven proposes were aimed at improving and modernizing nonproliferation laws to address new and challenging threats, restricting the sale and transport of nuclear technologies and equipment, closing the loopholes in the nuclear nonproliferation regimes that allow for states

---

[78] U.S. Department of Energy, "Remarks prepared for Energy Secretary Spencer Abraham," 26 May 2004 <http://www.energy.gov/engine/content.do?PUBLIC_ID=15949&BT_CODE=PR_SPEECHES&TT_CODE=P RESSSPEECH>.
[79] U.S. Department of State, "U.S. Wants to Intensify Global Nuclear Security Efforts," 26 May 2004 <http://usembassy.state.gov/mumbai/wwwhwashnews1874.html>.
[80] President George Bush, "Remarks by the President on Weapons of Mass Destruction Proliferation," 11 February 2004 <http://www.ndu.edu/info/whatsnew/PresBush-NDU.cfm>.

to illegally pursue WMD, and expanding the efforts to secure and destroy nuclear weapons and materials.[81]

The PSI, UN Security Resolution 1540, the Global Partnership, the Global Threat Reduction Initiative, and President Bush's February 11 proposals are all useful steps and antiproliferation measures aimed at countering the growing threat from nuclear weapons and related materials and technologies. However, there is a strong need for a global integrated approach to securing all HEU, plutonium, and other fissile and radiological materials to safeguard against illicit nuclear weapons programs, trafficking, and terrorism.

Need for an Integrated Approach

The current antiproliferation regime is much broader than the original Cold War construct, but various elements have developed independently. What is missing is a unifying construct, rationalizing and tying these efforts in an integrated approach to control the means and materials associated with weapons of mass destruction. High-level U.S. government attention is needed to address the problem.

Historically, the first step toward an antiproliferation regime can be seen in the traditional Cold War approach to arms control, characterized by various bilateral and multilateral agreements between the nuclear powers. Such agreements revolve around strategic nuclear arsenals and included such treaties as the 1963 Limited Test Ban Treaty, the 1972 Anti-Ballistic Missile Treaty, and the NPT, which entered into force in 1970. The end of the Cold War and the collapse of the Soviet Union necessitated an antiproliferation regime that could adapt to the changing strategic landscape. This landscape was dominated by the need to secure and eliminate weapons of mass destruction and related materials and technologies in the former Soviet Union. The Nunn–Lugar CTR program was the first post–Cold War adaptation of the traditional arms control approach and, as such, is the second stage of the antiproliferation programs and policies regime.

More recently, President Bush has initiated a third stage in this process by supporting a variety of multilateral initiatives, aimed at preventing the spread of nuclear weapons, materials, and expertise to rogue states and terror organizations. The Global Partnership, the

---

[81] U.S. Department of State, "Strengthening International Efforts Against WMD Proliferation," 11 February 2004 <http://www.state.gov/t/np/rls/fs/29293 htm>.

PSI, the Global Threat Reduction Initiative, and UN Security Council Resolution 1540, as well as the administration's targeted approach to specific countries of concern, including Libya, Iran, and North Korea, all contribute to this goal. However, these efforts have not achieved the synergy necessary to be greater than the sum of its parts. They are often implemented in a compartmentalized manner that does not permit the maximum benefits that could be gained from a holistic approach. UN Security Resolution 1540 comes the closest to providing an "organizing principle" under which all of the elements of an antiproliferation policy can be structured to form an integrated approach. Thus, UN Security Resolution 1540 should be used as the basis for enhancing both U.S. and international cooperation. If we are to achieve maximum results from each of these components, a way must be found to integrate them into a single, purposeful program.

Recent revelations about the extent and sophistication of the nuclear weapons black market led by Pakistani nuclear scientist Abdul Qadeer Khan has shed light on the increasing demand, by both terrorists and rogue states, for sophisticated nuclear weapons related information, technology, and materials. The recent plethora of international agreements on nuclear safety and security mechanisms, coupled with the understanding of the consequences of failure, make a coherent strategy achievable. Here, the experience of the CTR program could have its greatest value as the basis for achieving such an international consensus and effort.

XI. Conclusion—An International Imperative

Preventing rogue states and terrorist groups from acquiring nuclear weapons and related materials deserves the highest national priority. Cleaning up the nuclear legacy of the Cold War in the former Soviet Union remains vitally important—and urgent—if acquisition by terrorists of nuclear materials is to be blocked, but the threat of nuclear weapons proliferation is far broader in scope than just the former Soviet Union and must be addressed.

Even a state that is not actively pursuing nuclear weapons can be an unintentional source of proliferation, either of nuclear materials or of technologies related to weapons of mass destruction. A number of states have nuclear power plants capable of producing materials that could be diverted and used in some form of weapons-related device. Far more common are research facilities that have fissile materials that could be used in the manufacture of radiological dispersal devices. The United States should assign a high priority to ensuring that all these materials are properly safeguarded.

Seven broad conclusions can be identified from this review of problems and policies concerning nuclear terrorism and nuclear proliferation:

1. HEU is the material that could most easily be used by a terrorist organization to construct a rudimentary, but extremely powerful, atom bomb. Every effort should be made to prevent terrorists from acquiring this material because the frontiers of the United States remain quite permeable.

2. Important tasks remain to be accomplished by the Nunn–Lugar program in Russia. These include extending controls over fissile materials, securing tactical nuclear weapons, and disposing of excess plutonium. The obstacles are administrative and political in nature. High priority needs to be given to assuring the sustainability of Nunn–Lugar programs in Russia, both within the U.S. Congress and in the Russian government.

3. The techniques pioneered by the Nunn–Lugar programs could be applied in other cases beyond the former Soviet Union. Although Congress has approved this expansion in principle, only limited action has been taken. The administration has

begun to experiment in a limited way in Libya and Iraq with nonproliferation funds available to the State Department, but much more could potentially be done now.

4. India and Pakistan are not candidates for a large-scale Nunn–Lugar program. However, small beginnings, not necessarily with the direct involvement of the United States, could be undertaken that would enhance the safety and the stability of the nuclear rivalry between those two countries, as well as establish the foundations for a South Asian arms control regime.

5. Iran and North Korea have nuclear programs that are matters of grave concern to the international community. Friends and allies of the United States need to enhance their cooperation with the U.S. government in seeking to turn the two countries away from nuclear weapons. In that effort, several methods developed under Nunn–Lugar are potentially available and appear to have applicability to nonproliferation problems in Iran and North Korea. In the context of a settlement of these issues, and with the support of U.S. partners, Nunn–Lugar and related techniques should be applied.

6. New initiatives taken by the Bush administration have again emphasized the need for global cooperation in the antiproliferation effort. The G8's programs, the Global Threat Reduction Initiative, and UNSC Resolution 1540 could be coordinated to attack the problem of securing HEU and other nuclear material at facilities around the world.

7. As the antiproliferation campaign has intensified, it has become a more complex managerial program. The overall program lacks the degree of integration needed to make it as effective as it should be. Changes in the management of the government's antiproliferation programs are urgently required and should be carried out in connection with the reform of the government's intelligence functions called for by the 9/11 Commission.

Each of these points in itself is a major finding that must be pursued in the future. Together, they form the basis of a unified international effort to realistically deal with the threat of proliferation of nuclear weapons and materials.

The events of the past three years, although tragic in themselves, may present a window of opportunity for gaining international support for the application of CTR techniques and procedures on a broader scale as part of the effort of battling the spread of nuclear weapons and materials and their possible use by terrorists and nation-states. Recent terrorist acts, such as those in Madrid, Moscow, and Saudi Arabia, have brought home the points that no nation is safe from this threat and that if terrorists ever attain nuclear weapons, the results would be devastating. This realization should help individual nations to forget their parochial views and take a more international stance. Only through a unified effort can this threat adequately be addressed.

Acknowledgments

We extend our sincere thanks to the following people for sharing their expert knowledge and insights: Vic Alessi, Steve Black, Matthew Bunn, Tom Cochran, Scott Crow, Jo Husbands, Bill Hoehn, Laura Holgate, Dennis Kux, Rose Gottemoeller, Kenneth Luongo, Ken Myers Jr., Leonard Spector, Sharon Squassoni, Tom Wander, Anthony Wier, and Jon Wolfsthal.

www.ingramcontent.com/pod-product-compliance
Lightning Source LLC
Chambersburg PA
CBHW082150290526

45794CB00008B/3230